HALLMARKS

of THE SALVATION ARMY

A *FESTSCHRIFT*

(a volume of articles serving as a tribute)

to

General Eva Burrows (Rtd)

On her 80th birthday, September 15, 2009

HALLMARKS

of THE SALVATION ARMY

HENRY GARIEPY

STEPHEN COURT

FOREWORD BY

GENERAL SHAW CLIFTON

Crest  Books

Published jointly by Crest Books and the Austrailia South Territory

The Salvation Army National Headquarters
615 Slaters Lane
Alexandria, VA 22313

Major Ed Forster, Editor–in–Chief and National Literary Secretary
Judith L. Brown, Crest Books Coordinator
Richard Lewis, Designer

Phone: 703/684–5523
Fax: 703/302–8617

Available from The Salvation Army Supplies and Purchasing Departements
          Des Plaines, IL — 847/937–8896
          West Nyack, NY — 888/488–4882
          Atlanta, GA — 800/786–7372
          Long Beach, CA — 847/937–8896

Printed in the United States of America

Library of Congress Control Number: 2001012345
ISBN—13: 978-0-9792266-7-0

Unless otherwise noted, Scripture quotations are from the
Holy Bible New International Version 1978, used by permission
of Zondervan Bible Publishers.

MISSION STATEMENT

The Salvation Army,
an international movement,
is an evangelical part of the
universal Christian Church.
Its message is based on the Bible.
Its ministry is motivated
by love for God.
Its mission is to preach the
gospel of Jesus Christ
And meet human needs in his name
without discrimination.

The Salvation Army was born
To save souls
To grow saints
To serve suffering humanity.

~ General John Gowans (Rtd)

FOREWORD

GENERAL SHAW CLIFTON

I am delighted to introduce and recommend wholeheartedly this warm-hearted tribute to an outstanding Christian leader, General Eva Burrows (Rtd). This helpful book makes a most fitting tribute to a life of selfless service.

I have many positive memories of serving under General Burrows' leadership as a young officer doing legal work at International Headquarters in London in the 1980s. There were numerous occasions when she received me in her office, always with warmth and graciousness. I found in her a leader of vision, perception and principle. She was never afraid of making a clear decision. General Burrows was tough-minded when there was a need for that, and yet she was, and is, at all times a woman of Christian grace and warmth.

These chapters, written in her honour, will help and bless each reader. General Burrows would wish and pray for that to be the paramount outcome of any tribute paid to her. As you read and ponder, pause to give thanks for this inspiring example of a life dedicated to selfless service for Christ.

Shaw Clifton

General

London, September 2009

CONTENTS

CONTENTS

INTRODUCTION

COMMISSIONER JAMES KNAGGS

When you meet a person of high stature and significance, you make your own assessment of their integrity, character and contribution. If you then have opportunity to be associated with that person in an extended context, your perspective forms more concretely, and moves towards personal confidence. Such is the journey when you meet General Eva Burrows (Rtd). Rarely has a person in The Salvation Army gained respect and admiration of people around the world in such a very personal manner. To know and work with her is to be enabled and encouraged. To observe her daily, continuing contribution in the lives of people from all walks of life is to witness the grace and power of God through his humble servant.

Journey a day with her in this year of her 80th birthday. You're likely to start in the presence of God at an early hour, followed by a quick check of her computer for international emails that have arrived through the night. Undoubtedly, she will spend more time in prayer over what she has just learned, search through the news of the day on the web and set a plan to follow a very engaging schedule.

I expect that she might make a call or two from her BlackBerry to verify a few appointments and be on her way to her corps in Melbourne for a day of witness and support for others. The 'others' will include the corps officers, employees, volunteers and most assuredly the friends, sometime known as 'clients', all of whom will look forward to having a few words with this woman of God. In the middle of the day, she'll connect with the capital campaign chairperson who is helping to raise funds for the ongoing work of the 614 Life Centre and meet with the head of a major Australian business to ask for support. Many evenings are taken with service on the '614' bus that travels the streets and parks of Melbourne to minister primarily to the homeless youth of the city who cherish a few moments with 'Gen Eva'. Other days she would be found at the Training

College, teaching cadets studying to be officers in The Salvation Army. At the corps, she also conducts the recruiting class for people hoping to become soldiers in this movement of God.

General Burrows characterises the best of Salvationism with clarity and purpose. You can depend upon the veracity of her words and the depth of experience from which she draws. This comes presented in a graceful, yet authoritative approach that denotes respect towards the recipient and hope for their lives.

This work that you now hold in your hands is offered in honour of General Burrows with a substantive attempt to replicate the dynamic impact of the essentials in her life. You will hear from respected and admired contributors from around the world, with mission clarity and purpose communicated through their words and witness. The writers selected for this work bring together not only a global perspective, but a generational and gender-sensitive collection on subjects emerging today just as they have dominated our landscape through the years. We are blessed that General Shaw Clifton affirms this effort with his own words and support.

We are indebted to the editors, Colonel Henry Gariepy and Major Stephen Court, for putting together this landmark volume for the Army. The Colonel and the Major have made a great literary team, blending their skills to bring us this composite as a timely reminder of those hallmarks that define the mission of the Army. Although having never met personally, via the marvel of the internet they communicated across continents, establishing the book's format, recruiting the contributors and their responses, and preparing the manuscript for publication. The writers they have assembled speak eloquently on these essential attributes from their cross-section of geography, gender, age and experience. They have given us a book that lends itself for fruitful reading and discussion on our heritage and mission in this new era of change and challenge.

The subjects are important for all of us to consider. Our movement to win the world for Jesus is as firmly engaged as ever, with new inroads into cultures and practical service. This work brings to recollection our mission of 'The World for God'. Resonating within these pages is the confidence of 2 Timothy 1:12 (MSG), 'I couldn't be more sure of my ground—the

One I've trusted in can take care of what he's trusted me to do right to the end.'

General Burrows is the matriarch of the Australia Southern Territory, and deeply loved and esteemed around the world. We are pleased for the recognition that this book brings to her and how it points us forward in service to the honour and glory of God.

COMMISSIONER JAMES KNAGGS, a USA officer, was in 2006 appointed territorial commander for the Australia Southern Territory, and is the sponsor of this book. Commissioned in 1976, he and his wife Carolyn served as corps officers, and divisional and territorial youth leaders. Appointments followed as territorial evangelism and corps growth secretary, divisional commander, personnel secretary, and chief secretary. Of officer parents, he and Carolyn 'continually desire to intelligently discern God's will, enthusiastically follow his plan, and be used to bring people into God's kingdom'. They give testimony that God's grace has sustained them 'in both troublesome and triumphant times'. A hallmark of their leadership is their love and encouragement for others.

SECTION 1

TO SAVE SOULS

MISSION MUST MATTER

COMMISSIONER ISRAEL L. GAITHER

I believe God's calling of The Salvation Army is to participate in the bringing of the world under the influence and impact of his Kingdom. I believe it because of what I have experienced. And I am influenced by global leaders—among whom General Eva Burrows is foremost. This citizen Salvationist of the world embodies what it means to be a 'serving soldier'. The Burrows' mark is on the Army and its mission!

To serve the Kingdom effectively takes a confident certainty about what we are called to 'be' and 'do' as an Army of believers. 'Mission Must Matter' to every Salvationist!

Twenty-first century serving requires engagement in the mission with a clean heart. We are to serve as his holy, set apart people. The call to 'be' is urgent. Who knows how much more time we have remaining to engage this Kingdom warfare?

The growing demand for the Army's intervention is obvious. The global impact of poverty is massive, holding uncountable numbers hostage—with the children of the impoverished as the most vulnerable. Greed is consuming those who already have abundance, while those at the margins remain in despair.

What does it all mean for an Army of Salvation soldiers positioned around the globe with clean hearts and a clear vision; ready to serve and speak with confidence of our Sovereign God? It mandates that 'Mission Must Matter'!

SANCTIFIED SOLDIERS

There are imperatives that need to be acknowledged. The first and primary requisite is to grow an Army of sanctified soldiers. The primary objective in our soldier-making is to produce individuals who are striving to live in perfect love for Christ.

I have heard the plea all over the world: 'Lord, make us an Army of holiness'. It is the prayer of earnest Salvationists speaking multiple languages and dialects in every sector of this global enterprise. However, the truth is that our organisational systems and structures, the way we do things, will never reflect spiritual purity unless we who serve it are set apart followers. If 'Mission Matters' the Salvationist's unceasing passion is to know Christ.

When the work of The Salvation Army receives warm praise, it is not directed to an inanimate institution. The honour is given to people who make the institution come alive. Every soldier embodies 'The Salvation Army'. So it stands to reason that the first essential for the ensuring of a 'mission first' Salvation Army is to grow an Army of soldiers who are committed to his purpose.

MOBILISED TO SERVE

A second essential is to grow an Army of soldiers mobilised to serve. A sedentary band of satisfied soldiers will not result in mission effectiveness. Serving the present age demands a vast Army of competent, confident and courageous soldiers who show up in service to the mission. It is about 'serving'—not to 'be served'.

The urgent need of our time suggests that sitting in a pew on Sunday morning is not enough. Our worship must be rich and meaningful. It is the key in preparing a person for greater service. Nevertheless, an Army hall is just that; it is the place of preparation for service. The 'Army corps' is not a building. It is the collective body of Christ—set apart—to serve others with clear vision and clean hearts. This is not an Army of 'members'. And we dare not have Salvationists missing in 'serving' action. We are an Army of mobilised soldiers.

THE IDENTITY ISSUE

As I see it, a third mission essential is that we must settle the identity question. Consider the perception of 'who we are' by many in the population external to the Army.

Fifteen months after taking office in my present ministry assignment, I met with the leader of a prominent, faith-based, international human service agency. It was with ease that he described his clear understanding of the Army's role as part of the body of Christ. He knows we have congregations and he is well aware of our humanitarian work. In addition, he rejoices over the fact that America has a non-profit agency in which Christ is the centre point of everything we do. As I listened to him tell me 'who we are', I whispered a silent prayer that God would help us to remain true to his belief in us!

That evening I sat in a forum with a dozen other leading CEO/ presidents of the largest human service organisations in America. During a break in the proceedings, in a private conversation with one of the leaders who was familiar with our humanitarian work, she was amazed to learn that we have worshipping congregations. It was with genuine interest that she engaged me with deep questions about the ecclesiastical elements of our movement.

Those two conversations held hours apart on the same day reminded me again that America does not have a '20/20' view of who we 'really' are. In the Christian community we are a serving church. In the human service environment, we are a social service heavyweight.

But I am not worried about the dichotomy of perception of those external to the Army and who they believe we are. The greater concern to me is the attitudinal dichotomy that is held by some of us within the Army. I worry about congregations of soldiers who simply just want to be another church on another corner of their community, attending to human need as just another program on the schedule of weekly activities. That is a distortion of our mission.

I worry about our adequacy in the present when we have soldiers who wear the uniform as a sign of pride in an institution as opposed to a witness of our corporate purpose. If 'Mission Matters', we would rid ourselves of the notion of being satisfied with being understood to be just another church, or service club, or social organisation. There are enough already in the world!

We must settle the identity question. We are soldiers. We wear uniforms. And we fight against that which makes a person less than God intended.

Another essential is that we must not lose our heritage. As an African-American I am often reminded that the impact of my family's legacy on me is limited to just two generations. We dare not leave a historical vacuum to those who come behind us. An Army with a forgotten past will have a limiting influence and a diminished impact in the future.

There are two linked mission danger points to raise in this presentation. The risk of slipping away from our holiness heritage is one. I know of traditional holiness denominations that have this at the top of their agenda of organisational concerns.

A second hazard is the concern over the potential of losing our hymnology by the absence of the 'red song book'. It is especially apparent in Western society. Much of 'who we are' as a missioning people of God is spoken in our songs. If we lose our 'hymnology', we risk losing our 'mission theology'. We are the only faith institution I know that sings about itself!

When a soldier sings: 'I'm set apart for Jesus, his goodness I have seen. He makes my heart his altar, he keeps his temple clean. Our union none can sever, together every hour, his life is mine for ever—with resurrection power'…he or she is declaring their sanctified status for service.

We also must not forget our heroes. For they too remind us of the 'why' and 'worth' of this mission. Thank God that we still have some among us. General Eva Burrows stands in that long procession of those who have given sacrificial service for the sake of this magnificent cause.

We are inheritors of a cherished legacy, passed from generation to generation. It could be that the next one could determine whether our organisational heritage will continue to inform and press our mission purpose into their future.

A 'MISSION FIRST' ARMY

This is a plea for the necessity of a 'Mission First' Salvation Army on the march around the globe. It is a reminder that we have been called to rescue those at the margins who are held captive by circumstances that are an affront to God's intention for his creation.

We are an Army unafraid to live and serve the present age of any generation with love, grace and confidence; challenging the moral and spiritual sensibilities of any culture. I believe we are being called to reclaim our prophetic voice and presence.

What kind of Salvation Army is one in which 'Mission Matters'? A mission Salvation Army is restless. It is an Army discontented with the 'way things are'; preferring to work for 'what can be'. This is not the time to resign, give up, or take refuge within the walls of any citadel.

This is an Army with a clear vision of God's desire for his world. Despite the way things are, we believe this is still our Father's world.

We must remain an Army under divine orders. We are neither rooted nor rootless. This is a flexible movement that God can transplant wherever he so chooses. He can do with us what he pleases. We are at his service to participate in preparing the world to give it back to Jesus!

We are a disturbed Army. Yet, we are not discouraged. 'If it ain't broke don't fix it' is not an appropriate stance for this Army. Things may look alright—but it's all wrong if it is not under the Lordship of Christ.

A mission-focused Army confronts—and never conforms. We are risk-takers who take no pleasure in residing in comfort and convenience.

I am convinced that we do not need to reinvent this movement. What we need is Holy Spirit renewal. Eternity is at stake. The world must experience the Kingdom's transformative power. That is why mission matters so much to me! And by the way—'we win'!

COMMISSIONER ISRAEL L. GAITHER since 2006 has been national commander of The Salvation Army in the United States. Prior to that he served in London as chief of the staff at International Head-quarters, second in command of the worldwide Salvation Army, and as territorial commander for the USA East and South Africa. A powerful preacher of the gospel and articulate spokesman for the Army's mission, he is known as a man of God, a man with a message, and a man with a mission.

2

SALVATIONISM

COMMISSIONER HARRY READ

To the ever-expanding number of 'isms' in our language the second half of the 19th century seemed relatively undisturbed at the addition of yet another—Salvationism. Victoria, Empress Queen of the British Empire, continued to reign in her most regal way. Royal heads in Europe continued to wear their bejewelled crowns and, both in Europe and the rest of the world, political systems continued to function seemingly unaware that God had launched The Salvation Army into a needy world. If, however, among earthly powers there was little observable response, we who acknowledge the supremacy of spiritual powers believe that in heaven there was a ripple of excitement when Salvationism was born and, at the same time, a tremor was felt in hell's foundations. Salvationism is an unusual phenomenon: a spiritual force with a life-changing potential.

SALVATIONISM DEFINED

Before attempting to define Salvationism, let us consider what it is not. It is not a new creed, or a new set of organisational structures. It is not the product of a committee, or the brainchild of an entrepreneur. It is not the result of a survey or a public petition, neither is it a word held captive in 19th century concepts and practices.

The noun Salvationism takes us from the form to the substance, from the public perceptions of who we are to what we truly are. Symbols that Salvationists may well hold dear are not the essence of Salvationism either, because Salvationism is of the heart and all the good we are allowed to do proceeds from our hearts. That important statement resonates with our belief that, in the beginning Salvationism came, and continues to come, from the heart of God.

Salvationism is an engine-room kind of word, for within its robust, energy-exuding frame pulsates the heart of the Army. Here, the essential beliefs of the movement, its active, maturing and progressive concepts, its love and service-centred ministries, all reside in a living, quick-to-respond balance for the benefit of mankind. In an attempt to define further this word that probably defies total definition, we might consider it first and foremost as a word dependent on relationships: with God, with each other and with the community.

RELATIONSHIP WITH GOD

Salvationism has, from its beginnings, been predicated on a close, personal relationship with God. It was out of such a relationship that William Booth, a minister in the Methodist New Connexion Church, and his totally supportive wife Catherine had good reason to believe that he could fulfil his special evangelical gifts within that church. When, surprisingly, that opportunity was denied him, he and Catherine left the church with its security to accept an itinerant ministry, until such time as God opened up the way whereby their joint vision could be fulfilled. They took a great step in faith.

A while later, they took another step in faith when William said to Catherine in their home late one night, 'Kate, I have found my destiny'. In finding his destiny, William found Kate's also and their work in the East End of London commenced. Neither of our two first Salvationists doubted the nature of the Christ who, by his sacrifice, made salvation sure, and both were convinced of the work and person of the Holy Spirit. Salvationism, therefore, is rooted in an unmerited but deeply satisfying relationship with the Triune God. Salvationism would be a much less valued word were it not born of and continually sustained by this relationship.

KEY ELEMENT OF FELLOWSHIP

From the earliest of days, Salvationists, in their warm relationship with each other, have developed a family kind of fellowship that is one of the key elements of Salvationism. Ideally, what we have become in Christ is a vital part of our ministry. We know that there are times when the fellowship is less than ideal—a statement that is true of every fellowship. Even the New Testament Church in Corinth was not without its problems. However, Paul did not leave them to flounder and diminish but reminded them: 'Now you are the body of Christ and each one of you is a part of it' (1 Corinthians 12:27).

We are incredibly powerful when we are sharing fellowship with each other, praying for, and encouraging each other. Furthermore, our influence is greatly increased when, within the fellowship, we exercise those gifts of the Spirit we have been given to build up the Church as the body of Christ. Salvationism thrives in the relationships we have with each other.

REDEMPTION FOR THE COMMUNITY

Our Salvationism requires and helps us to relate to the wider community. William and Catherine had no doubts about their prime mandate—they were to win souls for the Kingdom and in pursuit of this great aim they held their meetings in a variety of unusual places including, of course, open-air meetings.

There was not much joy in the miserable streets of East London, but there was joy in abundance when sinners were converted. How could joy not be felt and expressed when sin had been forgiven? How could joy not be attractive to those who were still lost in their sin and longing to be free? Salvationists sang with faith and fervour. William Pearson's verses with the repetition of 'Joy, joy, joy, there is joy in The Salvation Army' was a song for those joyless, drab, discouraging days. The joy was the joy of the Lord; the corporate joy of the people called Salvationists; the joy offered to the joyless.

Did not our forebears in the faith stress also the sheer wonder of the scope of redemption? To those victims of poverty, abuse and addiction, the joyful Salvationists sang another of their hope-filled songs. Written by Richard Slater, the key line in the chorus offered so much: 'That can make a saint of a sinner'. In any context that is a staggering affirmation stimulating the question, 'Can God really do that?' And the answer had to be positive—yes, he can, will and does!

With inspired simplicity, William and Catherine maintained that there are no half measures in the gospel. The worst can become as the best: the unholy can become holy. It was heady stuff. The stuff of heart-hunger and impossible dreams all made possible through the unconditional love of the Father, the sacrifice of Jesus and the work of the Holy Spirit. Faith in a complete work of redemption is an integral part of Salvationism. From the destructive relationships in the community to the warm fellowship of God's people and to the heart of God himself new converts were led and began also to express Salvationism.

Booth was simply following the biblical concept of the people of God being the Body of Christ when, with creative common sense, he involved the converts in mission. To the question, 'Where will you get your preachers from?' he had replied, 'From the public houses'. In fact, his base was far broader than that. He took his preachers, witnesses and workers from every part of the fledgling movement. Booth was not slow to recognise the gifts of the Spirit in otherwise quite ordinary people, and encouraged their use. Little wonder those early days were marked by incredible growth! Much of the growth came, as it continues to come, through grassroots initiatives. God seems to like it that way.

Salvationism inevitably leads to service within the community. It has always been so and, no doubt, will continue. Salvationists of all ages are engaged in these ministries. Remarkably, many Salvationists have opted to leave the comfort of their family homes in order to live in deprived inner city areas to live out the gospel either formally or informally. Salvationism? Of course!

INSPIRED RESOURCES

Salvationism is best expressed in those lives who model its attributes. For those of us privileged to know as a friend, and to work with, General Eva Burrows, her life and leadership resonates as a radiant illustration of the profound meaning of Salvationism. She is a complete Salvationist, and her international leadership superbly modelled Salvationism. We are grateful to God for the General's natural expression of Salvationism.

What then of other Salvation Army characteristics? Our music is God's gift to us, as are our Leagues of Mercy, community groups and our work with the homeless and disadvantaged. God gave us the will and resources to bring people into a relationship with us in order that they might enter into a relationship with him.

All the big words of Christianity find their place within this engine-room word, Salvationism: unconditional love, sacrifice, forgiveness, grace, acceptance, faith, hope, intercession and burden-bearing. Each distinctive word blends with the others to make Salvationism real in us in order that God's eternal purposes might be achieved.

S A L V A T I O N I S M
(A gift from God's heart)

From my own heart I make this gift to you—
A gift of unconditional love and grace.
If to my heart-to-heart gift you are true
You will more often seek me face to face.

Your fellowship with one another will
Reflect my love and joy—my focus on the Christ:
Your mutual care and prayer will help fulfil
The plans for which my Son was sacrificed.

Go, in my name, claim your community:
The sad, the weak and each aspiring soul,
Let Pentecost be your authority—
Tell them and show them, I can make them whole.
Salvationism is a word of power
And your Commission for this crucial hour.

COMMISSIONER HARRY READ in 1942 at age 18 volunteered for military service and was trained as a wireless operator for the 6th Airborne Division, with the mission of liberating Europe. In the very early morning of D-Day, he parachuted into France, an unforgettable experience! In 1946, still on military service, Harry experienced the call to officership. He and his wife Win served in the UK at corps, training college, IHQ, divisional leadership, as chief secretary in Canada, and territorial leaders for Australia Eastern and the United Kingdom. Following retirement in 1990 he authored *Words of Life* for 10 years. Win was Promoted to Glory in 2007 and with a reduced schedule the Commissioner continues to fulfill his calling.

3

THE WORD OF GOD

COMMISSIONER LALKIAMLOVA

'In the beginning was the Word, and the Word was with God, and the Word was God.' With these words the apostle John launched his mighty gospel. From the beginning of creation, the Word that proceeded from God shaped, controlled and directed the whole movement of creation. As recorded in the first chapter of Genesis everything that was formed in the creation came forth by the Word of God. The first man and woman, Adam and Eve, lived by the Word of God in the Garden of Eden. God called Abraham, Isaac and Jacob and directed all their movements by his verbal words.

Until the time of Moses the Word of God was not in any written form. God called Moses and gave him Ten Commandments for his chosen people with instructions to put them in writing and hand them down to the generations to come. He called prophets for special purposes and gave them his words to be conveyed to kings, rulers and ordinary people. No legitimate prophet would dare to convey the Word of God as their own or add any word, but they communicated the Lord's Words to the people as they had heard them. They uttered 'Thus said the Lord'. Both Isaiah 51:16 and Jeremiah 1:9 record, 'I have put my words in your mouth.' The authenticity of their words in time was justified with fulfilment.

As time went on the Word of God that had been verbally handed down from generation to generation was prepared in written form and such writings are accepted as inspired by God and as infallible.

JESUS AND THE WORD OF GOD

In the beginning of his earthly ministry, although being the Son of God, Jesus was led by the Spirit into the high desert mountain to be alone and to be tempted by the devil. He was there for 40 days and 40 nights without taking any food or drink. He was hungry and weak and might well have been looking for something to eat to sustain him on his return to the village. At this very moment, when Jesus was exceedingly vulnerable, the devil appeared and began his mission to tempt Jesus. First he tried to tempt him to turn the stone into bread. But our Lord was armed with the Word of God. Responding to the devil's temptation he quoted from the Scripture in Deuteronomy 8:3: 'Man does not live on bread alone, but on every word that comes from the mouth of God' (Matthew 4:1–4).

This is the foundation of our belief. Bread may satisfy our physical hunger but it is the Word of God that gives life to those who believe in him. Jesus considered the Scripture as the living Word of God and used it to resist the power of Satan, saying 'It is written'. The writer of Hebrews 4:12 says, 'The Word of God is living and active. Sharper than any double-edged sword, it penetrates even to dividing soul and spirit, joints and marrow; it judges the thoughts and attitudes of the heart.'

THE SALVATION ARMY AND SCRIPTURE

The Salvation Army, as a Bible-believing Church, puts the Scriptures first in its 11 articles: 'We believe that the Scriptures of the Old and New Testaments were given by inspiration of God, and that they only constitute the Divine rule of Christian faith and practice'.

In the midst of doubt and questions on the authority and authenticity of the Scriptures, the Army finds many reasons why we believe that they are written with the inspiration of God. God's leading in the history of the Israelites, fulfilment of the words of prophets, evidence of events of the Bible, the teaching and use of the Scriptures by Jesus, and the inspiration that the Scriptures have to individual believers, all speak of the divine inspiration of the Word of God. We also believe because in the Bible we find God drawing near to us as revealed in Christ and declaring to us the way to our salvation and conduct as the children of God.

Concerning Christian faith and conduct, the Salvationist does not accept any other writing or authority as equal to the Bible. We also believe that Jesus is the Word that became flesh and dwelt among us (John 1:14). The Army, from its inception, put this theology of incarnation into practice. General John Gowans' articulation of the Army's maxim as 'saving souls, growing saints and serving suffering humanity' lives out this sacred truth.

The Army proclaims that our belief that the Scriptures are the Word of God is inscribed in our Articles of Faith and by putting its truths into action. This belief finds vibrant expression even by our songs, such as the following written by Salvationist Will Brand:

Set forth within the sacred word
The path of life is plainly shown;
The ways of God its lines record,
For every soul of man made known,
The truth, of all our hopes the ground,
Is here within its pages found.

The Word of God is not only to be believed but lived. It is a lifeline for believers. Salvationists examine themselves to ensure that they truthfully hold on to the Word of God. The true Salvationist loves the Word of God, is nourished by it, reads it continually, lives by it, and shares it with others.

General Eva Burrows has been to us a beautiful example of the Salvationist as a person of the Word of God. She has lived it, taught it, preached it, and derived its guidance and inspiration for her worldwide ministry for God and the Army.

Our prayer, as it relates to our first statement of faith affirming our belief in the inspiration of Scripture, is that our lives and service may 'adorn the doctrine'.

COMMISSIONER LALKIAMLOVA was born in Mizoram, India. As a teenager he became a freedom fighter, hiding in the jungle, carrying weapons, with absolute loyalty demanded. At age 18 he attended The Salvation Army and heard God say, 'I want you to work for my Kingdom, not an earthly kingdom, to point people to Jesus—true freedom is to be found in him.' He knelt and promised to serve the Lord for the rest of his life. He was captured by the Indian military authorities and severely beaten. To his surprise the commander said, 'If God has called you, then I must release you.' He and his wife Lalhlimpuii served in various appointments in India, including as territorial leaders of the India Central Territory. In 2003 he was appointed international secretary of the South Asia Zone. His full story is told in *Unsung Heroes* published by Salvation Books in 2007.

4

EVANGELISM

CSM PHIL WALL

'In school we were repeatedly told that God didn't exist.' Nothing in my upbringing, the child of Salvation Army officers dwelling in a culture still claiming to be 'Christian', equipped me for what I was hearing. Sitting in the quarters of Lieutenants Geoff and Sandra Ryan—recently appointed Salvation Army officers at St Petersburg Corps in the newly-opened Russian Command—I tried to take it in. As Vadim, a published poet, member of the Russian intellectual elite and the new Corps Sergeant Major continued, my Western mind repeatedly attempted, and repeatedly failed, to make the leap into the old atheistic Soviet worldview. In this state, even God's name was designed to terrify the masses; in Russian, the word for God is, 'bog', as in 'bogeyman'.

Meeting Vadim and serving in this archaic culture undergoing enormous transition became a watershed in my life. Preaching the gospel in this strange and foreign post-perestroikan land changed my vocation forever. As such, I remain grateful to those made the visit possible; the UK territory, my fellow campaigners from the UK Mission Team and Geoff and Sandra Ryan who, while not knowing us, put us up and put up with us. Over the past 20 years I have served in many territories around the world but when it comes to 'specialling' few assignments have been as special as that trip.

To this end I am also indebted to General Eva Burrows for the lasting impact we received in going to St Petersburg. Were it not for her decision to return our movement to Russia, I would never have got to learn from Vadim and his comrades. And as hard as it was to understand the context that we were in, it would have been impossible to predict how this cross-cultural mission trip would equip us for ministry back in the UK.

If you had asked me upon boarding why I was going to Russia, I would no doubt have talked about the prospective evangelistic opportunities, the privilege of preaching the gospel and the great honour of joining, if but temporarily, The Salvation Army's frontline forces as they strove to do what Napoleon and Hitler could not do by invading Russia. In retrospect I am grateful to General Burrows, The Salvation Army and Geoff and Sandra Ryan because those 10 days behind the fallen Iron Curtain changed my life and have shaped my ministry ever since.

In his book, *In Darkest England and the Way Back In*, Gary Bishop masterfully retells the story of how he along with a team of young Salvation Army church planters moved into a deprived community in East Manchester. He tells of a stunning moment of revelation. In a minute, all of his missionary motivations and expectations unravelled. It was then that Gary realised that God hadn't brought him to Manchester to change Manchester after all. Rather, God had called Gary to Manchester so that he could change Gary. Anyone who has experienced authentic mission will recognise this revelation. We commence our call to change the world only to discover that the mission field first calls us to change. In my experience this first missionary lesson takes a lifetime to learn.

As Vadim described a country which banished God from public life, a state-approved church riddled with KGB agents and a people with little or no knowledge of the gospel story, I grew increasingly aghast. This godless society appeared virtually untouched by the Enlightenment, Reformation or Evangelical revivals. If it wasn't for his obvious intelligence and eloquence I would have found the whole thing utterly incredible. And yet now, not long after, I have experienced these same feelings so many times without ever having to leave the comfort of my own country.

Having served as a full-time evangelist for two decades, more recently my calling has carried on in the world of business. Here, there is a similarly inverse proportion between the sheer number of opportunities to share Christ with those I work with and, in turn, their general level of ignorance when it comes to the Christian story. And if it weren't for that afternoon in St Petersburg, I would be less prepared for the conversations I now share on a daily basis. Here, in the once Christian West, many have little or no knowledge of God and are frightened of allowing him into their personal, let alone public, life. The God whose story, laws and revelation provide the infrastructure of Western civilisation, not to mention much that she is most proud of, has seemingly been shooed away. The unwanted bogey-man of a secular, know-better-world, God is either an embarrassing myth or a dangerous and divisive device.

For those of us trying to reach a post-Christian world, pre-Christian Communist Russia has much to teach us. I'm not sure when the lights of Christendom will finally be turned off or, for that matter, who will flick the switch. But what is clear is that we who call ourselves evangelists are increasingly operating in a post-Christian context. While we may be keen to remain 'Christian', the same cannot be said of our culture or our contemporaries. We would do well then to learn the lessons of those Salvationists commissioned by General Eva Burrows in the Communist aftermath. It may then be possible for us to boldly go into a post-Christian world and proclaim anew the good news of Jesus.

Through much of our discussion with Vadim, one question was left hanging. 'In a State which continually told its people that God didn't exist and where to mention the word was to invite the bogeyman into the room, did people stop believing in God altogether?' Having finally been asked the question, Vadim revelled in a knowing laugh.

'Of course we believed in God,' he said. 'After all, if God didn't exist, why did they spend so much time warning us about him? It makes no sense to be so threatened by fiction or fantasy.' With hindsight, Vadim's response appears increasingly familiar. In secular 21st century Europe people are not shunning the transcendent or losing their religions. In fact, while some things go in and out of fashion, spirituality is permanently in style in the post-Christian West. To this end, the real challenge for the Church is no longer to be clever or culturally relevant enough but to be spiritual enough. Our societies have not been suckered into the gospel according to secularism. Our neighbours are not dead to God or lacking in spiritual appetite. Rather, they are hungry for authentic experience but sadly no longer look to the Church to satisfy this.

Vadim's Russia and my United Kingdom have the same hunger in common. Far from satiating our hunger for meaning, the consumption-driven culture of Western life has left many famished for meaning and starved for fulfilment. These are indeed challenging days for evangelists in the West. But the challenge is not a lack of opportunity. The doctrine of materialism has been tried and found wanting. As an investment banker once said to me, 'I go to work every day and earn all this money but I can't think of one good reason why.' Whether it's a Russian poet after the collapse of Communism or a wealthy banker in the midst of capitalism, every human needs something to live for. Christians everywhere and throughout history know that the gospel answers this question, satisfies this hunger and leads to fullness of life. Hence both in a first century village in Palestine and again in the 21st century global village Jesus declares that, 'The fields are white unto harvest'.

Unfortunately the wealth of missionary opportunity in the West is being met by a Church which is impoverished in terms of self-confidence. We appear unconvinced by the transforming power of Jesus, unsure as to his ability to make all things new and unmoved by the possibilities and challenges ahead. If we are to win the West again it will take a more convicted and confident Church than we see at present.

As the evangelists we encountered in St Petersburg understood, we worship a God who cannot be deleted or edited out of our corporate consciousness. He is not a God who needs an invitation but a God who is unrelenting in his efforts to win his creation and redeem his people. As a mystic once wrote, 'We worship a God who is constantly lapping at the shores of people's lives.' Like the tides of the oceans, our God breaks over our secular shores and revisits his image-laden creation. In the same way that the Iron Curtain proved porous to the Spirit of God, the cultural barriers of the post-Christian West cannot hold back the One who creates and sustains all things.

I remember asking Vadim what it was like to live in such a godless State. He smiled and answered, 'They held up their hands to block the sun, but the light broke through.' If we wish to shine God's light in the darkness of the post-Christian West and reach this secular yet spiritual generation, then we can learn much from our Salvationist brothers and sisters who confidently revealed the atheistic sham at the heart of communist propaganda and boldly pointed to the One who is the Light of Life. It's time for us to raise our own hands to the Son who has shone on our world and without whom we cannot survive or thrive. By sending those Salvationists into Russia, General Eva Burrows not only took on the bogeyman but began to teach us how to win the West.

CSM PHIL WALL is the son of officer parents. As an evangelist he has worked out that calling in such diverse contexts as a London policeman, Army mission team leader and most recently as a business entrepreneur. While working for the  Army he founded a number of initiatives including the Roots Conference and the international Orphan Charity Hopehiv. He is part of the leadership team in London that in 1994 planted a corps where he serves as corps sergeant-major. He spends most of his time coaching senior leaders and building social enterprise within the corporate world as well as creating resources for Orphans in Africa. He and his wife Wendy are proud parents of three children.

5

YOUTH

COMMISSIONER VIBEKE KROMMENHOEK

Long before the end of the 20th century when mission strategies, statistics and church growth reports documented the importance of youth and children's outreach and ministry for the growth of the local church, 'we' in The Salvation Army already 'knew'. We knew that youth and children should not just be included, but be prioritised in bringing Christ to the world. Two important sources on which we base this 'knowing' are Scripture and our tradition.

In the Gospels, both in teaching and in attitude, Jesus demonstrates that youth and children matter in God's Kingdom. Just look at how he includes the children, when mothers ask him to bless them. Or read how he takes the questioner seriously as the rich young ruler struggles to find a direction in life. And notice that Jesus feeds the multitudes because of a young boy's willingness to share his limited food supply.

General William Booth, writing about India, urged his officers to pay not only 1,000 times more attention to the children, but 10,000 times more attention to the children. As one of seven priorities for her second term in office, General Eva Burrows listed 'youth and children'. She expressed the hope that she would be remembered as a General for youth. In her life and ministry General Burrows models the importance of youth and children; many are the examples of this in her authorised biography *General of God's Army*.

Our present General, Shaw Clifton, emphasises too the importance of reaching the children, when he says 'Our primary purpose is, and always has been, to introduce men and women and girls and boys to Jesus Christ.' These are just a few examples of how past and present leaders communicate that 'children and young people are a high priority in the Salvation Army mission'. The emphasis on the importance of youth and children is evident both in Scripture and The Salvation Army's tradition. Also, reliable church growth reports repeatedly show that 80 per cent of all vibrant and church-committed Christians have made a decision for Christ before the age of 25 years. But, as I said at the beginning, we already knew that.

However clear the examples are from Jesus' life and teaching, the signals from The Salvation Army's top administration, and the evidence of statistics, in the end it is at grassroots level that youth and children have to be reached with the gospel. Only where there is local motivation and passion embodied in the vision for mission carried by local leaders and children's workers will children be reached by the Spirit. The expression 'God's vision will never lack God's supply' has, in such a context, been shown to be true over and over again.

In the corps at Turku, a town on Finland's west coast, children's work was at rock bottom at the end of the 1980s, and youth work was non-existent. In the past the young people's corps had been flourishing and had also been the starting point of a lifelong journey with the Lord for several Finnish officers, but now this all belonged to the past. Finally eight years ago, a young single officer managed to get the children's work off the ground again. Today several of the children have become junior soldiers and their parents, adherents or soldiers. The gain has not only been children, but whole families. When the young captain was asked by her leaders how she did it, she answered spontaneously: 'I just said to God, "I can't live without a Sunday school for children"—and the rest is history.' Passion for youth and children is one of the most important motivators for growth, and it still takes only one person who possesses that to start a children's ministry.

Five years ago General John Larsson appointed me to commence The Salvation Army's mission in Poland. As a beginning I interviewed colleagues who in the past had been involved in starting the Army's work in former communist countries in Eastern Europe. I asked them all what they would do differently today, if they were given the chance to start all over again with the experience they now had gained. One of them answered: 'I would start youth and children's ministry. That is what I should have done from the very beginning; I was far too occupied with reclaiming former Salvation Army property and starting social work. I believe that is why today we still have hardly any children and committed young people in that region and, as a result, only a very small group of national Salvationists'. Where, in the former Eastern Bloc, The Salvation Army's holistic mission flourishes today, the vast majority of those places have a past where the first pioneers placed all their eggs in the youth and children's ministry 'basket'. History shows that this was a wise decision, affecting both long-term effectiveness in mission and growth in numbers of national soldiers.

'Where would Jesus be?' is a quote I recently found, which actually is a very good variation on the previous 'What would Jesus do?' Where would Jesus be when it comes to youth and children's ministry today? If we want to reach the unreached children, one very good option is to go and be present where they are. Don't let us stay behind thick walls in our own buildings, with fancy programs catering only for children who are from 'several' generations of Salvationists. Let's be with the children at the shelters for single parents. Let's go to the playgrounds and sports fields. The reputation of a church that meets a need without first having to spend ages on committees and reports considering whether they should act or not, a church that is creative and resourceful, driven to move out—what happened to that attitude in our youth and children's ministry?

Sports ministry is today an upcoming and effective way of being with children and meeting them where they are in more senses than one. Or going weekly to the local playground and organising games and activities is another way of being both present and relevant where children are. We can, with our presence, in some kind of clearly-identified SA clothing, show that the children are safe, and at the same time communicate to their parents that, as long as we are around, someone is watching over them. These kinds of methods contain two essential values in the first steps of offering the Good News to the young people of today, the values being 'God is good' and 'Christians are okay'.

But the children have to be offered more than fun and fellowship alone. The corps has to make sure that Christ himself and his values are presented, for example in a 'cool' Sunday school setting, with Youth Alpha material. Discipleship training can and should start early in order to help young people get on the right track from the beginning. Junior soldiership, taught in junior soldier and corps cadet classes, is, in our tradition, the form in which we share and teach children commitment to discipleship and the beauty of holy living. For the Kingdom's sake and The Salvation Army's future, this should continue be a priority, for example, in forming specially designed cell groups for this age group, using relevant and creative communication methods. In the 21st century, we are about to deal with the children and grandchildren of the prodigal son—young people who have hardly heard about and surely never felt touched by the loving arms of a heavenly Father. If we don't reach them and offer them a sound foundation in Christ, the children of today will never have the choice of building their lives on the Solid Rock.

I dare to state that any corps alive, vibrant and shining its light in the local community and being effective in engaging in the holistic mission of The Salvation Army, will evidence a successful youth and children's ministry. The importance of having a ministry that meets the local children where they are and takes them by the hand, teaching them about Jesus and showing them his attitude, cannot be emphasised enough. Issues like the 'right' or 'wrong' style of worship should not be on the top of our corps council agenda. If they are, we have got something essentially wrong. When at the top of our agenda is how we may communicate Jesus better to the grandchildren of the prodigal son, making sure we are where Jesus Christ would be, then I am certain the Holy Spirit will reveal his will and lead us. It is only perfect, if it works locally.

COMMISSIONER VIBEKE KROMMENHOEK, of Danish origin, with her husband Dick, entered the International Training College and they were commissioned in 1983. They have served in the Netherlands, Denmark and France. In their tenure at IHQ she was appointed international youth coordinator. From 2005 to 2008 she was responsible for the start of The Salvation Army in Poland. She and her husband presently serve as leaders of the Finland and Estonia Territory.

6

MEDIA MINISTRY

MAJOR WILLIS HOWELL

In the mid-1400s Johannes Gutenberg knocked over the first domino in what would eventually become a worldwide, insatiable drive to communicate with an ever-widening audience by developing the movable metal type printing press. His process revolutionised the world with the ability to mass produce the written word. The age of mass communication through media was born.

Before going any further, let's be sure we share the same understanding of the basic premise of the subject. The term mass media refers to any format or technology medium that allows a message to be communicated to a large mass of people. In very broad terms, our world today is impacted by eight various mass media which have developed over the centuries since Gutenberg got the ball rolling: books, which soon led to newspapers, that led to magazines; recorded sound, which paved the way for radio; movies, that set us up for television. All of this is dwarfed, however, by what is now perhaps the most limitless and significant media format in all of history that combines the best of all previous media into something completely new and far more influential—the internet. Communicating a message that has a decidedly religious intent to it—such as religious instruction, outreach, or evangelism—by means of any of these media has come to be called media ministry.

From the beginning, The Salvation Army has always had a drive to do whatever was most effective in reaching the greatest numbers of the public as possible in order to advance our mission and communicate the gospel message. Taking the lead of our founders, the early Army intentionally shunned 'church and chapel ways' in favour of learning to speak the language of the common man's culture. We chose to meet people where they were and where they gathered rather than expecting them to come to us. This led us to embrace the practice of preaching in saloons and dance halls, as well as open-air street meetings where brigades of Salvationists would unflinchingly go into neighbourhoods infested with crime and violence.

This desire to reach and minister to the greatest possible number of people also brought us to the understanding that media technology would allow us to throw our nets far wider than the simple sound of our voices and bands. We could impact an even greater audience if we could learn to leverage our message through the power of media. As a result, at various points throughout our existence, the Army has used every medium of mass communication available for the purpose of advancing our ministry and broadcasting our message. We developed an active and often very creative interest in media ministry, occasionally even pioneering cutting-edge media.

Understandably, we started with print media—the most widely effective medium of the day—and prepared handbills, tracts, sensational posters, newspapers and magazines. But the effective use of these simple media tools drew attention to our message. Vast crowds were attracted as a result. In the high profile case of the 'Maiden Tribute' exposé, partnering with media mogul W.T. Stead and his widely-read *Pall Mall Gazette* helped the Army's voice to be amplified in such a way as to eventually cause social outrage when it shone an unwelcome light on the largely ignored child sex industry of Victorian England.

There were also the books. Booth's classic *In Darkest England and the Way Out* was hugely successful in reaching masses of people with his ideas of salvation for body, mind and soul. In fact, the book completely sold out of the first edition run of 10,000 copies the first day it was made available in 1890, sold out the second run of 40,000 books just a month later, and ultimately sold over 100,000 copies—a runaway bestseller in its day.

Around the same time a world away in Melbourne, Australia, the Army learned to speak a new and innovative media language. Salvationists went out on the leading edge of available media technology and began communicating the gospel to thousands through moving pictures. The Limelight Department brought The Salvation Army into the movie-making business even before Thomas Edison established what is recognised as the world's first actual motion picture studio in 1893.

By 1910, audio recordings were available of William Booth delivering short evangelistic messages, and the Army was a regular feature of commercial radio broadcasts by 1922. In the 1950s, convinced of the huge outreach power of the increasingly popular medium of television, the Army took the incredibly bold step of producing a regular television series. Through *The Living Word,* the Army broadcast the gospel into the homes of viewers serviced by some 75 TV stations across North America in the '50s and early '60s. In order to have the greatest impact on its audience, no corners were cut in the quality of the production. In fact, the Canadian-produced series was 'ahead of the market'—according to General Arnold Brown, who had served as the show's producer—in that it was filmed entirely in colour. This was years before the colour broadcast format became the standard for the television industry.

Why the quick look back over our shoulder? Simply to point out the courage and vision the Army has displayed throughout the years by embracing whatever is the most current and effective language of communication technology for the sake of reaching and evangelising the masses. Intentionally making use of media for ministry purposes is in our DNA.

Today we have available to us what is arguably the most revolutionary and far-reaching medium to date—the internet. If books and print media were compared to the horse and buggy, the internet would compare to intergalactic travel at warp speed. The virtual communities of cyberspace have become this culture's gathering place, and online communication has become the common man's language of the 21st century. Through internet access, the world is literally at our fingertips—or at least our keyboards.

Through a smorgasbord of web-based methods, communication with multiple thousands all over the world can be easily accomplished with little or no significant financial burden. Information about a limitless number of subjects can be easily accessed through 'search engines' such as Google or Yahoo within a few keystrokes. Countless web logs ('blogs') offer social comment, observations and opinions on a seemingly infinite variety of subjects from the silly to the serious. YouTube, the online video phenomenon whose own branding statement declares 'Broadcast Yourself', explains something of the scope of their mission when they announce on their website that, 'Everyone can watch videos on YouTube. People can see firsthand accounts of current events, find videos about their hobbies and interests, and discover the quirky and unusual. As more people capture special moments on video, *YouTube is empowering them to become the broadcasters of tomorrow.*'[1] (emphasis added). This is to say nothing of social networking sites such as Facebook, where you can even find General Eva Burrows, or have the ability to share audio and video files via podcasts, or streaming audio/video, and so much more that is available as viable opportunities of media ministry. Incidentally, General Burrows, who is media savvy, has been viewed preaching the gospel by over 30 million persons worldwide in a series of three telecasts.

So where is the Army in all this? While we've mastered previous media languages, are we adequately speaking the media language of 21st century culture in order to purposefully advance our mission to the world? What message are we hoping to get across to today's generation by posting videos of our brass band concerts on video-sharing sites? What result are we looking for? How are we embracing and leveraging the staggering possibilities of ministry through this medium?

While there is no way to accurately count them, there are easily hundreds—perhaps even thousands—of individual Salvationists throughout the world who have developed into fluent online communicators, 'cyber missionaries', if you will. As such, they've become quite effective at reaching incredible numbers of people who would never darken the doors of an Army corps. They've seized on the significant ministry possibilities of the internet by offering passionate, mission-laced opinions, essays, journals, audio/video files and commentaries in ways which would make our innovation-driven forebears proud. Army 'bloggers' generally weigh in on current events, societal trends, issues and concerns of the day. They offer their take on these matters and many more from a bold, unapologetic, Salvationist perspective. Their passionate and often well-reasoned postings are frequently punctuated with Scripture, and it's not uncommon for early Army writers to be quoted or pointed to as examples.

Actively ministering through this medium to unseen thousands, the roll of current Salvationist bloggers includes a few territorial commanders,

---

[1] YouTube website; Company History, http://www.youtube.com/t/about

retired commissioners, staff officers, corps officers and soldiers. General Shaw Clifton even gets into the act having established The General of The Salvation Army website (http://www.salvationarmy.org/thegeneral). Even more, the General uses the communication power of the internet to send out a pastoral e-letter, written 'from time to time', intended to share the various matters on his heart directly to Salvationists throughout the world.

Counts of the 'hits' on these sites—the times that someone purposefully visits one of them to check out the content—can number well into the hundreds of thousands over a year. Popular though 'unofficial' Army internet destinations such as www.armybarmy.com, www.therubicon.org, beyondthebrook.blogspot.com and www.flocksdiner.com, to name just a few of what may be the more popular sites, would easily be reaching multi-thousands per month. A prime example of a website is 'Journal of Aggressive Christianity' started in 1999, with over 60 issues to date. Its readership exceeds periodicals of most territories and enjoys contributions from soldiers to generals.

Through his personal website that includes a blog page as well as a weekly podcast feature, a Salvation Army officer in the southern US has reached an unduplicated count of 19,926 distinct people in the first six months of his site being made available. How does that compare to the number of *War Cry*s that get passed out over six months where you are? In that same six-month period, his site received 143,027 visits. What does that tell us? It tells us that, while the corps he is appointed to may be small, by taking advantage of today's media possibilities the reach and impact of his ministry is significant far beyond the local community where he serves.

The Army's 'Wonderful Words of Life' radio broadcast—available on 1500 radio stations worldwide—has been going out over the airwaves for more than 50 years and has received countless reports of conversions over the years. While some would be content to leave it at that, the producers of the program recognised the possibilities of reaching even more people by making the show available via the internet. A monthly average of nearly 1400 online listeners now log on to OnePlace.com to hear the program whenever they choose.

A quick look elsewhere online proves that most, if not all, territorial and many divisional headquarters—as well as a number of large metropolitan commands and even a significant collection of local corps—have active, attractive, official websites. Essentially all of these sites present general information and engaging pictures relating to what the Army is doing in that command area. Readily seen, clearly placed links make it easy to sign up to volunteer, donate financially, and find out how to receive social service-related assistance. All very helpful.

But take another look at the website of your corps, command, division or territory. Based on what you see, ask yourself these questions:

• While the medium used may adequately speak the language of today's media culture, does the message clearly communicate concern for the *soul* as well as the body?

• Does it give the impression of an Army of people who merely *do* good things for others, or does it also make unmistakably clear the message that through Jesus one can *be* good?

• Does it reflect the passions and priorities of heaven as much as the practices of good public relations?

• Is the core message of salvation through Jesus Christ lost in the medium—relegated to a small, easily overlooked link on a sidebar, or drop-down menu—or is it boldly displayed for all to see and find?

You see, clearly sharing the hope that is available in Jesus isn't merely part of our message—it *is* our message. And the innovative, well-crafted use of media in all its languages and formats will ensure that we broadcast that message far and wide.

MAJOR WILLIS HOWELL, training principal for the USA South, is a second-generation Salvationist. He grew up living in varied locations, including Morocco, Africa. In college he majored in music education, and joined the Navy in 1975, becoming a member of the Navy's premier travelling Show Band and the Navy Academy Band. With his wife, Barbara, a fifth-generation Salvationist, they served in corps, youth and divisional leadership. From 1991 to 2008 he hosted The Salvation Army's international 'Wonderful Words of Life' radio program and currently writes a blog at www.always-burning.blogspot.com. In June 2007 he was appointed president of the Army's Evangeline Booth College, and principal of the School for Officer Training, in Atlanta.

7

PREACHING THE WORD

GENERAL BRAMWELL TILLSLEY (RTD)

The challenge to preach the Word is deeply embedded in Scripture. The Apostle Paul wrote, 'God was pleased through the foolishness of what was preached to save those who believe' (1 Corinthians 1:21). He added, 'Woe to me if I do not preach the gospel' (1 Corinthians 9:16). Dr Roger Green wrote: 'It is beyond question that the great revivals of the church, beginning with the Church in Jerusalem, came by the power of the Holy Spirit through the proclamation of the gospel and such continues to be the case now.'

In the Christian Mission, corps were called preaching stations, giving evidence of the importance of preaching in our beginning history. Evangeline Booth suggested preaching is the main job in the Army. Bramwell Booth said of his father, 'It is as a preacher of Jesus Christ and his salvation, that the Founder will be most remembered in all the lands he visited.'

Speaking to the contemporary church, Martyn Lloyd-Jones wrote, 'I would say without any hesitation that the most important need in the Christian Church today is true preaching.' John Stott added, 'I believe in preaching and I further believe that nothing is better calculated to restore health and vitality to the church, and to lead its members into maturity in Christ, than a rediscovery of true, biblical contemporary preaching.' The translator of Helmut Thielicke's *The Trouble With the Church* wrote in the preface, 'Wherever we find, even in this day, a vital, living congregation, we find at its centre vital preaching.'

Perhaps we can with profit consider some of the marks of effective preaching. First of all, it commands attention. It stimulates the mind and penetrates the heart. It avoids the danger of becoming merely a script reader. An Irish woman, after hearing a bishop read his discourse remarked, 'Glory to God, if he can't remember it, how does he expect us to?' The little girl who said to her pastor, 'It is exciting to hear you preach' paid him the highest of compliments.

Preaching employs a simple, straightforward vocabulary. 'Clear, direct, simple' was the way Bramwell Booth described his father's vocabulary. This does not imply 'talking down' to people. Preaching down never lifts up.

It was Charles Spurgeon who wrote, 'It is not enough to be so plain that you can be understood. You must speak so that you cannot be misunderstood.' James Denney's comment is worth heeding. 'Don't preach over people's heads, for the man who shoots above the target does not prove thereby that he has superior ammunition. He just proves that he cannot shoot.' John Wesley suggested that preachers may think with the learned but must speak with the common people.

Effective preaching must be solidly based on Scripture with an up-to-date application. In a series of articles on preaching, the Founder wrote: 'Anticipate the character of your audience. If you are a stranger, inquire. It would be ridiculous for me to go on speaking to people as to their duty without knowing their condition.'

Salvationist preachers would do well to emulate the highly effective preachment of General Eva Burrows. Her biographer, Henry Gariepy, records, 'Burrows has the skill of modulating her message to her setting and audience. She is a master of illustration, often introducing something of local or topical interest in response to the needs of her hearers. When serving in the Third World she said, "I do not preach Christianity, I preach Christ." Christology is the heart of her theology and preachment. And so it must be for all of us who stand behind the sacred desk.'

Effective preaching is the outcome of good preparation. The Founder's personal secretary wrote of him: 'His thoroughness was never more in evidence than in the preparation of his addresses and sermons. Draft after draft would be prepared until he was satisfied that the form was accurate and the language was sufficiently expressive.'

Preparing to preach as well as preaching itself is hard work. When a young student suggested that preaching never made him tired, the bishop responded, 'Son, when a man preaches, somebody gets tired.' Charles Swindoll wrote, 'If you hear a good sermon from your minister, it isn't because he is creatively shooting from the hip. Count on it, it is because he is doing his homework.'

Charles Jefferson, a former pastor of Broadway Tabernacle in New York added: 'The work of preaching is the most difficult of all the things which a minister is called to do. It is at once the most strenuous and most exacting of all forms of labour. It requires a fuller combination and a finer balance of powers than are required in any other department of human effort.'

God's Word is proclaimed with ardour, passion and zeal in the power of the Spirit. Both the message and the messenger are important. Here of course we need a balance. Sometimes we pray, 'Hide the speaker behind the cross' but there is a sense in which the speaker should not be hid. Preaching has been described as 'truth through human personality'. Both the personality and the truth are important. When the message concludes, however, the people should not feel 'how great is the preacher' but rather 'how wonderful is Jesus'.

Someone asked Spurgeon how they could communicate with people and reach them as he did. 'It is very simple,' he said. 'Get on fire for God and people will come to see you burn.' Such is good counsel for our preachment in the Army.

Historically in the Army our preaching has led up to a time of decision. We preach for a verdict. Our preaching is not merely to instruct or edify, though it is that, but to bring men and women to a decision on the most momentous question that can engage the human mind. The 'passion for souls' remained with William Booth until the day he went to be with the Lord. After a wonderful meeting, a young officer, seeing the General was very tired, tried to do something to cheer him up. He enthusiastically spoke of the meeting—the crowds, the singing, the long procession at the Mercy Seat. 'Yes,' said the General, 'but did you see that other procession, those who were going out of the hall, out into the night without Christ?' We must always preach for a verdict.

Perhaps the weakest part of our preaching is the transition from 'proclamation' to 'invitation'. Assuming this is the case, a few suggestions may be in order. The invitation should be but an extension of the sermon. We should make some application as we move through the message. The congregation should be prepared for what we are going to ask of them.

It is helpful to inform the organist/pianist what songs or choruses we plan to use, if in fact you use a song or chorus. The songs should be well known and pitched in a slightly lower key. We should resist changing the songs or choruses. There should be a real warmth in the invitation and it should not be forced. Our task is to proclaim the Word; it is the Spirit's work to bring about a response.

Yes, preaching the Word is a vital part of our heritage. Martyn Lloyd-Jones reminds us, 'The work of preaching is the highest and the greatest and the most glorious calling to which anyone can ever be called.' This adds credence to what Emil Brunner, the noted Swiss theologian wrote: 'Where there is true preaching, where in the obedience of faith the Word is proclaimed, there in spite of all appearances to the contrary the most important thing that ever takes place upon this earth takes place.' Let us not lose by default or neglect, but maintain the priority of the proclamation of the gospel so souls may still find Christ at our altars. We thus join with Charles Wesley:

Happy, if with my latest breath
I may but gasp his name,
Preach him to all, and cry in death:
Behold, behold the Lamb.

GENERAL BRAMWELL TILLSLEY (RTD), a Canadian, is the son of Salvationist parents. With his wife Maude they served as corps officers, provincial and divisional commander in Canada, principal of the International Training College, chief secretary in the USA Southern Territory, territorial commander in Australia Southern, and chief of the staff. He earned a BA in Philosophy. In 1993 he was elected General. Ill health brought early retirement. Preaching the Word has always been a hallmark of his ministry.

8

PERIODICALS

DR ROBERT DOCTER, OF

Booth knew how to attract attention. His open-air street meetings used brass instruments—they were a big part of the British culture, and they were loud.

His publications attracted attention as well. They had loud headlines and a strong message in relation to the cultural issues of the day. Even the title of his principal publication, *War Cry*, shouted a message.

The venerable *War Cry* has been around for almost as long as there has been a Salvation Army. First published in December of 1879, it provided bold headlines for a text-heavy vehicle to inform and educate new soldiers on specific matters pertaining to the Booths' philosophy and theology. It also discussed pertinent social issues of interest to the general public as well as spreading the good news about Army growth.

As the Army spread internationally, the *War Cry* editors translated the title into the national tongue and published their own material for their local readership. According to the 2009 Yearbook, 53 territories or commands today list this publication. The words, still sung, of William Howard Doane's song, 'Ever is the war cry, victory, victory', speak of its enduring quality.

With a strong desire to communicate effectively with particular readers, gradually more publications appeared. In 2009, International Headquarters publishes *The Officer, All the World, Global Exchange* (replaced in January 2009 by *Revive*) and *Words of Life*.

The United Kingdom Territory adds to this *Salvationist, Kids Alive* and *The War Cry*.

Internationally, most of the world's territories have perceived a need to communicate more effectively—primarily with soldiers and friends. Their publications often had different titles in different territories. This growth has continued in spurts, with a major growth period beginning in the

1980s through to the present day. These publications seem to have focused on specific reader classifications, age grouping, language, gender. They differ in size, number of pages, style, purpose, number of issues published per month, paper stock and manner of distribution. They seem to develop different personalities, often similar to that of the editor.

They are all periodicals—a publication appearing at regular intervals for a specific readership on behalf of its sponsor.

Any periodical has a distinct audience and a specific purpose. When a periodical is published by an organisation, it tends to become the 'voice' of the 'company'—a 'house organ'. Some see this term negatively because they perceive the purpose of the house organ to be limited to publicity. It doesn't have to be that way. While the publication might speak for the 'company' and advance themes that both aid and please the publisher, the house organ might still be visually appealing, well-designed, sharply focused, occasionally critical and speak to readers about matters that interest them. In other words, the 'house organ' can still be 'professional'.

Salvation Army periodicals like the *War Cry, Salvationist, New Frontier, All the World, On Fire, Priority* and, according to the 2009 Yearbook, about 150 other publications, are clearly written to communicate aspects of the 'company'—the Army. They are 'house organs', advancing the cause and the mission of the organisation. In recent years, the line between the historic Army house organ and a more sophisticated, professional publication has blurred. Many of the Army publications birthed in the last few decades are highly professional.

There are criteria to consider by any house organ on the road to professionalism. The first of these, I believe, is to develop an identity. Where identity confusion exists, the publication's inconsistencies make it a difficult read. Identity has to do with values, self-image, style, culture, purpose and readership.

Second, after the staff and the publisher have a complete understanding of the publication's intended identity, a clear set of goals and objectives needs to be identified. Without that foundation you have no identity.

I'm responsible for leading publications in the USA Western Territory. Our 'flagship' is *New Frontier*. We endeavour to achieve professionalism. Our identity is that of a Salvation Army tabloid-size newspaper. We emphasise stories that relate to the Army's mission, and strive to make a story newsworthy even if it describes past events.

New Frontier has always had one primary goal and one ancillary purpose. Our goal: to publish timely, readable and visually appealing news and feature stories about the Army's march toward mission fulfilment. Please note, the first word in our goal statement is 'timely'. We focus on the reader and print material we believe the reader would want to read about the international, national and territorial Army. Our ancillary purpose: to provide opportunities for two-way communication between readers and territorial leadership through transmission of timely information directly to homes. This includes soldiers, employees, advisory board members, donors, friends of the Army and key Army leaders throughout the world.

Additional objectives include to communicate our perception of the essence of the Western, national and international Army to itself—what it is, what its ethic and ethos requires, its areas of strength and areas in which it needs to improve. We encourage innovation by giving new ideas visibility, and publicise creative ways to implement traditional programs, promote world service giving, attendance at special events, and nurture spirituality.

While examining an article for publication, the first criterion for any editor is to ask: 'Will anyone read this? If so, who? If not, why not?' It is essential that we know as much as possible about our readers.

PRINT AND ELECTRONIC MEDIA TENSIONS

Some see tension these days between print and electronic media—between newspapers and internet news sites like Google and web logs (blogs). The computer-driven internet is international, fast, void of printing costs, more voracious in its demands to be fed, and able to accommodate longer material sources. It is here. It is used. It is important to become skilful in its use. It can broadcast to the world as well as to the 35 soldiers of a corps.

Must we see these media forms as competitive—in conflict? No! Many of our web designs to date appear somewhat amateurish. We need designs similar to those published by other religious groups, churches and organisations. Our 'information architecture' is lacking. Very often, too many of us are not timely, leaving material sitting on the web unchanged for weeks. This drives people away. We must improve our ability to maintain people's interests with more timely presentations.

Some of our periodicals some day might perform more effectively on the web. But we don't know. Most of the decision-makers of the Army are unprepared to make this judgment. We need experience and then the willingness to modify some periodicals for web publication totally. Some publications fit more easily into this notion of mutuality.

General Eva Burrows was always a great encourager to me personally, and to the progress of Army publications. She initiated the International Literary Council from which emerged the first International Literary Conference, a landmark literary event coordinated by Colonel Henry Gariepy.

For those of us who seek to advance the Army and proclaim the gospel by periodicals, the words of Isaiah are as a glove thrown at our feet: 'See, I am, doing a new thing! Now it springs up; do you not perceive it?' (Isaiah 43:18–19). Salvationists of an earlier day set for us the example. Let us perceive the new opportunities God has for us, and rise up to the challenge of proclamation in our day.

DR ROBERT DOCTER is founding editor of *New Frontier Publications*, along with *Caring*, and *Nuevas Fronteras* for USA Western Territory. He served for 40 years as corps sergeant-major of Pasadena Tabernacle Corps, 62 years as bandsman, marched 51 times in the Rose Bowl Parade, 'held forth' for years at open-air meetings, and teaches an adult Sunday School class. He earned his BA degree in English and his PhD in Educational and Counselling Psychology. From 1960 until 1998 he taught at California's State University as a professor of educational and counselling psychology. As an emeritus professor he teaches graduate classes. In 1969 he was elected to the Board of Education of the Los Angeles School District, and was chosen president in 1975. He is a licensed psychotherapist. His book of popular columns, *A View from the Corner*, was published in 2008. In 2005 he was admitted to the Order of the Founder.

9

FULLNESS IN CHRIST

LIEUT-COLONEL JANET MUNN

'You have been given fullness in Christ
who is the head over every power and authority'
(Colossians 2:10).

FULLNESS OF TIME

Slowly sinks the reign of darkness,
Yielding to the Saviour's day,
When the slaves of sinful bondage
Cast their evil chains away.
Upward, Christward, homeward, Godward!
Millions who are now afar
Shall be brought into the Kingdom,
Where the Father's children are. —Albert Orsborn

My grandmother experienced some fantastic prayer meetings at The Salvation Army in Canada. But that was in 1915! To hear people talk today, sometimes it sounds as though God was actively at work doing powerful deeds only back in the good old days. It could seem as though a lot of the best stories of his works are from a long time ago.

Quite the opposite is true. From the beginning the Lord has planned for a progressive, cumulative increase in the knowledge of God on Earth. We see this principle in the natural realm. Scientists don't start all over again with their research in each generation, but rather build on the discoveries and understandings of previous generations. This is true in medicine, the arts, communications, transportation and so on. One generation builds upon and adds to what the previous generations have experienced, discovered and come to know. This also is true of the reality of God among his people.

God's first instruction to Adam and Eve was to 'be fruitful and increase' (Genesis 1:22). God repeatedly promised increase to the Israelites through Moses, through Jeremiah and Ezekiel. In the infant Church there was evidence of increase—as 'the word of God continued to increase and spread' (Acts 12:24).

Increase toward what? Habakkuk wrote: 'For the time will come when all the earth will be filled, as the waters fill the sea, with an awareness of the glory of the Lord' (Habakkuk 2:14 NLT). That's where planet Earth is headed! All this increase—in knowledge, in technology, in communications, in population—is leading to a time of fullness, in the fullness of time.

FULLNESS OF SALVATION

Full salvation, full salvation,
Lo the fountain, opened wide,
Streams through every land and nation
From the Saviour's wounded side!
Full salvation, full salvation,
Streams an endless crimson tide.   —Francis Bottome

There is no escape for those who neglect this great salvation (Hebrews 2:3). Jesus taught us to boldly declare for his Kingdom to *come*! And regarding his will, that it *be done*! Right here, now, on Earth, in our lifetimes, as his will is being 'done in heaven'! That's praying for fullness in Christ, for which Jesus suffered to provide a great and full salvation. The full price has been paid for the fullness of our salvation.

FULLNESS THROUGH EMPTINESS

'Does God call you? Go and God will be with you…and as the years speed by you will increasingly thank God that no business prospects, no fond friendships, no lust of power or love of scheduled ease kept you from the battle's front with its burdens and bitter conflicts and fierce sorrows and soul-satisfying triumphs' (*Heart Talks on Holiness*, Brengle).

'Then Jesus said to the disciples, "If any of you wants to be my follower, you must put aside your selfish ambition, shoulder your cross, and follow me. If you try to keep your life for yourself, you will lose it. But if you give up your life for me, you will find true life'" (Matthew 16:24–25 NLT).

Jesus Christ laid aside the power and glory due only to God, to endure being fully human, in frail flesh, vulnerable to human cruelty, hatred and violence manifest at his crucifixion. The Apostle Paul reminds us in Philippians that because of Christ's self-sacrifice, God the Father exalted him to the highest place and that he is now and forever worshipped and ultimately everyone will acknowledge his honored position. But that is not the reason, not the motivation for which Jesus Christ suffered—we are the reason. We are our Lord's inheritance. The motivation behind his self-emptying was you.

INTERGENERATIONAL FULLNESS

Catherine Booth reminds us, 'Day by day you must labour to wake up your children to the realisation that they belong to God, and that he has sent them into the world, not to look after their own little petty, personal interests, but to devote themselves to the promotion of his, and that in doing this they will find happiness, usefulness and glory' (*The Training of Children*).

Generations are interconnected. In Psalm 78 we see the Lord's intention for one generation to pass on the knowledge of God to the next. This is his design. If ever there was a list of generations that are interconnected it is the patriarchs—Abraham, Isaac and Jacob. God often describes himself as their God, the tri-generational God, the God of the generations, the God of Abraham, the God of Isaac and the God of Jacob.

Even in retirement General Eva Burrows models this Kingdom principle in her life. She supports the youth events in her territory. She sits among the youth during the loud praise and worship music and stands as a worshipper right alongside them. The younger generation recognises her love for them and reciprocates with the warm greeting, 'Gen Eva'! What an example she is of the heart of the spiritual parents turning toward the heart of the sons and daughters.

FULLNESS — PROMISE OF GREATER THINGS
What a work the Lord has done
By his saving grace;
Let us praise him, every one,

In his holy place.
He has saved us gloriously,
Led us onward faithfully,
Yet he promised we should see
Even greater things.
Greater things! Greater things!
Give us faith, O Lord, we pray,
Faith for greater things. —Albert Orsborn

'God had provided something better for us, so that apart from us they should not be made perfect' (Hebrews 11:40 NASB). The writer uses the word 'better' over 10 times in comparing the old covenant to the new. God the Father, through Jesus Christ, has provided a better hope (7:9), a better covenant (7:22), better promises (8:6), better sacrifices (9:23), better possessions (10:34), a better country (11:16), a better resurrection (11:35), and in summary, just a big 'something better for us' (11:40).

'Now to him who is able to do immeasurably more than all we ask or imagine, according to his power that is at work within us, to him be glory in the church and in Christ Jesus throughout all generations, for ever and ever!' (Ephesians 3:20–21).

INTERNATIONAL FULLNESS

O boundless salvation! deep ocean of love,
O fulness of mercy, Christ brought from above.
The whole world redeeming, so rich and so free,
Now flowing for all men, come, roll over me! —William Booth

God expanded the 'circle of inclusion' through the Hebrew people, beginning with Abraham, to whom God promised, 'I will bless you…and all the peoples of the earth will be blessed through you' (Genesis 12:2–3). Jesus Christ commissioned and empowered his Church to go as witnesses to all nations, making disciples as they went—from Jerusalem, Judea, Samaria and to the ends of the Earth.

This God-community is always reaching, stretching, growing, expanding, embracing in joyful love. This is evident in the life of Eva Burrows as well, leaving her homeland in obedience to the divine call to take the gospel to the far reaches of the Earth. Her internationalism demonstrates the very heart of God in this regard.

At the end of human history those gathered around the throne of God are from all nations, and every tribe, language, people and race are present. This is the heart of God. All people. All nations. Every language. Every race. All gathered to himself. A Father celebrating having all his children home. A joyful bridegroom delighting in the beauty of his bride for whom he has long awaited and prepared. This is the fullness of the redemption of the world for which Christ died. Nothing else will do. William Booth saw the heavenly vision—'fullness of mercy…the whole world redeeming… now flowing for all…'

'He is the atoning sacrifice for our sins, and not only for ours but also for the sins of the whole world' (1 John 2:2).

LIEUT-COLONEL JANET MUNN is the secretary for spiritual life development for The Salvation Army (as well as associate principal of the International College for Officers and Centre for Spiritual Life Development) and is serving in London, England. She trained as a Salvation Army officer in the USA Eastern Territory. She finds the Bible the most invigorating, disturbing and enlivening thing she has ever read and  is endeavouring to live in the light of it. She has completed her BA and MA degrees as well as M.Div. requirements and is currently enrolled in a Doctor of Ministry program in spiritual formation at Ashland Theological Seminary. She is the daughter of a Nazarene pastor-father and a disciple-making mother, the wife of an Anglo-American egalitarian husband, and the mother of two beautiful, articulate and blessed young adults.

SECTION 2

TO GROW SAINTS

10

HOLINESS

GENERAL SHAW CLIFTON

What a daunting word is 'holiness'. Yet for those committed to Jesus Christ it has profound significance. It tugs at us. It beckons us. Every time we hear it we feel dissatisfied, as though some unreachable goal is being dangled before us. Holiness…ah, yes, holiness…that to which we are called, even to which the Scriptures command us…and yet it seems so far away.

Can we ever be holy?

The answer is yes! To start with, the moment we are saved we become holy, in the sense that we are then and there changed into Christ's person. All that he has is holy. All those set apart for him are holy. We know this because Paul in his New Testament letters (for example Romans 16:2, Ephesians 1:18) refers to all the believers as 'saints' (Greek: *hoi hagioi*, literally 'the holy ones'). The book of the Acts of the Apostles does the same (Acts 9:13; 26:10).

Yet we also know that these same believers, these 'holy ones', were very far from perfect. Time and again Paul feels the need to offer rebuke. There is hardly a letter of his that does not do this in one form or another. So 'the holy ones' had holy status in Christ, but their personal lives often looked quite different from what we associate with the word 'holiness'.

Clearly then there is frequently a gap between our holy status in Christ and our everyday behaviour. Growing in grace is about narrowing that gap, the gap that leaves us discontented. General Frederick Coutts described this feeling as one of 'holy discontent', teaching us that it was planted within us by the Holy Spirit precisely to draw us onward and upward into increasing Christlikeness. In other words, this sense of discontentedness ought not to discourage us, but instead it is to be used positively to bring us closer to our Lord.

Closeness to Jesus will result in greater likeness to him. He is unique, and yet he invites us to imitate him. This sounds unachievable until we remember that he gives himself to us through his Holy Spirit indwelling each believer. As we open our hearts to receive him more and more, the more like him we can grow.

There comes a moment for each of us when we realise that, though we have faith and are saved, we do not yet have victory over temptation. To put it simply, we are saved and still sinning. There comes a moment of crisis, often quite some time after we have accepted Christ, when it dawns upon us that our new-found status in him needs to be matched by our thoughts, words and deeds, daily, hourly, even moment by moment. When this happens we have reached a crucial milestone in our spiritual walk. We have been led of God to recognise our need to go still deeper into the things of Christ, into his purity, his holiness, his indwelling. Suddenly we experience a hatred for sin in all its manifestations, large and small. Suddenly we focus as never before upon Jesus. Suddenly we hunger and thirst after righteousness and purity. Suddenly the Scriptures become still more passionately the object of our searching minds and hearts. All this is a beginning in the sanctified life. We have stepped out on the quest for the blessing of a clean heart.

Countless believers can testify to this experience. They describe it as a further step in faith, speaking of it as though it were as vivid an experience as coming to Christ in the first place for salvation, for forgiveness for past sins. Now their focus is upon their future sins. They are tired of being saved but sinning. They are determined no longer to settle for second best, for that repetitive, enervating cycle of sinning and repenting, sinning and repenting. They see with blinding clarity that when Jesus died he purchased for us much, much more than that. The salvation he provides through Calvary's cross is full and comprehensive, taking us onward into the sanctified life, a life of holiness.

From such a new beginning, from such a turning point (Greek: *crucis*, 'crisis') there flows a Holy Spirit guided process, often called growing in grace. It involves steadily closing that gap of discontentedness between our holy status in Christ and the reality of the lives we live. Day by day, our purity is enhanced, our closeness and likeness to Jesus grows, and our hatred for sin deepens within. Our worldly ambitions fade. We become more obedient to the will of God. As the songwriter Helen Lemmel said:

Turn your eyes upon Jesus,
Look full in his wonderful face,
And the things of earth will grow strangely dim
In the light of his glory and grace.

The holy life is not one of moral or sinless perfection. We still make mistakes and get things wrong. We are still capable of hurting others inadvertently. The word 'sorry' is a crucial part of the holy life. It is the hankering after sin that has gone now. Sin has lost its attractiveness for us.

Holiness of life is not an optional extra for a believer. At its heart is obedience to God and the will of God. Without obedience there can be no spiritual maturity. The walk of holiness centres upon seeking out God's will for us. He is there to guide and to control once we surrender. He guides through his word in Scripture, through prayer, and through the wise counsel of mature Christian friends and leaders. Obedience is the key to progress in the faith.

Let no-one think that holiness of life is dull or that experiencing the blessing of a clean heart robotises your God-given personality. Far from it! Your sense of humour will be enhanced, but now it is clean and pure. Your insights into people will deepen, and you will appreciate them more and more, despite seeing their human flaws and foibles. That great preacher and teacher of holiness, Commissioner Samuel Logan Brengle, said that the blessing of a clean heart improves your judgment—about people, about situations, about key choices to be made.

Holiness also renders you more effective in mission for Christ since it not only empowers you for compassionate service in his name but also transforms you into a more attractive (and attracting) person whom others wish to emulate, to the point of asking about your Saviour. A holy life is a powerful soul-winning thing. An unsanctified life can wrestle to deploy all kinds of evangelical tools and initiatives but will in the end have to admit defeat. There is no substitute for purity of heart, a heart filled with the perfect love of Christ. Others see it and are intrigued.

If obedience is at the heart of the holy life, it is closely accompanied by humility. There can be no holiness that is proud or boastful. In 1 Corinthians 13 we are taught that love 'does not boast' and 'is not proud' (13:4). The humility of Christ is imparted to the waiting, sincerely seeking child of God. This humility is not self-abasement. We are not called to behave as though we are doormats on which folk can trample, but we are called to treat others as better than ourselves, to have respect and esteem for all around us, and to remain forever teachable in the things of Christ and his gospel of love.

Obedience and humility need love, Christlike love, as their rich soil if they are to prosper within us. Again 1 Corinthians 13 comes to our aid. Love is at the root of the holy life. So in closing let us paraphrase for a moment some of the words from this most famous of New Testament chapters and see afresh what holiness looks like:

> Holiness is patient, holiness is kind. Holiness does not envy, does not boast, is not proud. Holiness is not rude, is not self-seeking, is not easily angered, keeps no record of wrongs. Holiness does not delight in evil but rejoices with the truth. Holiness always protects, always trusts, always hopes, always perseveres. Holiness never fails.

Love is indispensable because Jesus is indispensable. The indwelling of the Holy Spirit is indispensable because the Holy Spirit is the Spirit of Jesus. The holiness, the purity, of Jesus is indispensable. When we seek, we surely find.

GENERAL SHAW CLIFTON, LLB, BD, PhD, AKC, before his election as General in 2006 had served on five continents. He led the Army through a period of significant growth in the Islamic Republic of Pakistan and faced the challenges of secularism while leading the Army in New Zealand. With his wife Helen he also served as corps officer in the British Territory, in corps and a secondary school in Zimbabwe, and as divisional leader in the USA. From 1982–89 he was Legal and Parliamentary Secretary at IHQ. In June 2004 he and Helen became leaders of the Army in the United Kingdom. He has authored six books, including *New Love* and *Who Are These Salvationists?*

11

LOCAL OFFICERSHIP

DR (RETIRED CSM) BRAMWELL SOUTHWELL

'Now all of you together are Christ's body, and each of you is a separate and necessary part of it' (1 Corinthians 12:27 NLT).

In the earliest days of the Christian Mission, William Booth's vision was to bring the gospel to the unchurched masses of England. God used Booth's gift of evangelism to achieve extraordinary results as people sought salvation. It was his intention that converts join local churches, but there were difficulties. Booth said, 'They would not go where they were sent, they were not wanted when they did go, and I soon found that I wanted them myself.'

At the time, he did not know that the embryo of a worldwide movement was in the process of formation. For God wanted The Christian Mission to grow, eventually becoming The Salvation Army. The original converts brought others, and they came in increasing numbers.

Using John Wesley's model, Booth encouraged the establishment of groups of believers who would be accountable to each other in their spiritual service. He wanted everyone to accept a part together as Christ's body. Classes and wards were formed and clustered geographically into stations. People were found who could be entrusted with supervision of converts and accountability. Booth insisted that 'every station should have a treasurer and a secretary'. Women were used to visit converts in their homes and were known as 'shepherdesses'. Booth's criteria were that all leaders be 'lovers of souls, living holy lives'. The emphasis on evangelism remained. The Spirit of God guided and empowered the enterprise, and the rest is history.

With the establishment of the quasi-military structure of The Salvation Army (1878), stations became corps. The model of officership and soldiership developed. In the corps the rank of non-commissioned officer was introduced. Later, this changed to local officer. The positions of treasurer and secretary were already in place. The term sergeant was given to the leader of a ward, company or band. Other terms such as watchmen, registrars, adjutants and even sick stewards were identified, each with a distinctive role. None of these titles was retained. Gradually, further additions and refinements occurred, and in 1904 a list of 14 senior local and four junior local officer positions appeared in the *Orders and Regulations*:

> **Senior**: treasurer, secretary, sergeant-major, recruiting sergeant, corps cadet guardian, bandmaster, quartermaster, publications sergeant-major, ward sergeant, colour sergeant, band sergeant, sergeant, envoy and ward publisher; **Junior**: junior sergeant-major, young people's legion secretary, Band of Love leader, junior soldiers' treasurer. A local officer was issued a warrant defining the duties and responsibilities of the position.

A definition of a local officer might be 'one who can get others to work together'. Booth's guidelines match well with the criteria listed by Paul in 1 Timothy 3:2–3. The principal features required of such a person are to have a right relationship with God, understand his purpose, and accept his truths as revealed in Scripture.

Booth had a penchant for wanting to know what was happening among his people. Written reports from the field to headquarters included those from sergeants, and were often published in the weekly bulletin, *The War Cry*. Years later, when writing of the fully-fledged Salvation Army, Commissioner Railton commented:

> There naturally arose a system of reporting and inspection which enabled the General to ascertain, with remarkable accuracy, how far his wishes were being carried out, or neglected, by any of his followers. He sometimes said, 'I would like, if I could, to get a return from every man and every woman in The Army as to what they do for God and their fellow men every day.'

Booth clearly saw himself as directly accountable to God for every action undertaken by any soldier of The Salvation Army.

The Founder needed troops on the ground who could take initiative. An excellent example of this is to be found in the commencement of The

Salvation Army in Australia. In May 1880 immigrants John Gore and Edward Saunders met at a Wesleyan Methodist Church in Adelaide. They discovered that each had earlier links with The Christian Mission under Booth. Within weeks they had established a station on their own with other like-minded people. In effect, these acting local officers were in place before official approval had been secured. It was not until the following year that officers arrived from London to take charge of the new corps.

What of the present and the future? What does a corps of the 21st century look like? Key words to be found in the formation of growing fellowships are flexibility, thinking 'outside the square', innovation. Each corps can represent a visible response to local needs. Whereas The Salvation Army will retain many of its traditions, it will not be bound rigidly by them. Even the term 'local officer' may be undergoing change.

In some areas role descriptions of leaders are crystallised into titles such as facilitator, financial counsellor, small group leader, worship leader, pastoral care counsellor. Instead of a traditionally constituted corps council (management group), it may now include a mix of key local officers and other facilitators who have oversight of worship, discipleship, mission, ministry, young people and administration. Each gives time, skills and a unique experience of God's redeeming grace as a volunteer without expectation of monetary reward. The impact of their example and enthusiasm upon this multi-faceted ministry is immeasurable. To remain with Paul's metaphor in 1 Corinthians 12, they represent the joints, muscles and sinews of the organisation.

A difficulty facing many local officers today is the issue of how to manage time pressures. A person's employment can make huge demands on available time. Family responsibilities can exert a heavy load too. There are often physical, mental and spiritual health considerations which need to be addressed. In 1983 I took the role of corps sergeant-major at the peak of a busy professional life. For me the decision to do so was fraught with uncertainty. Yet, many years earlier, I was promised that 'God has not given us a spirit of fear and timidity, but of power, love, and self-discipline' (2 Timothy 1:7). It is a matter of much gratitude that God's faithfulness was experienced over the 22 years that followed. There were times when work prevented my participation in a corps activity. In whatever the situation, time and time again the assurance remained that I was where I should be. The belief that God's grace is sufficient in every circumstance came in a fresh manner as I learned of *The Sacrament of the Present Moment* (Caussade). This has become a treasured enduring principle, as it must be for so many others.

A century after William Booth's death in 1912, local officers of The Salvation Army respond to his charter to see the work done, souls saved, and the world brought to Jesus. Today, 130,828 local officers worldwide are committed to the Army's mission to 'preach the gospel of Jesus Christ and meet human needs in his name without discrimination'. Each has a unique story, but each a common purpose. From time to time the Army recognises the exceptional service of a Salvationist with its highest award, the Order of the Founder. Local officers are to be found among more than 200 recipients of the award since 1917.

During the 16 years since her retirement in 1993, General Eva Burrows served faithfully as a soldier in the corps of Camberwell in the eastern suburbs of Melbourne, before transferring to Melbourne Corps Project 614 and giving sterling service as recruiting sergeant at this exciting, innovative, relevant force in a resurgent Salvation Army centre in Melbourne's CBD. The ministry reaches into a kaleidoscopic mix of street people, office workers and business leaders of this city. It is here that General Eva responds to God's call for her.

As chairperson of the 614 Advisory Board she assists in strategic planning of the corps. Her people skills are actively employed among those who attend the Sunday services and outreach activities during the week. Burdened people find acceptance, love and security through her ministry. On the same day General Eva may meet with leading citizens, yet soon after be speaking on behalf of a defendant in a court hearing. On several occasions she has travelled a 200 km round trip to visit a person in prison. She counsels converts in her role as recruiting sergeant, encouraging their growth towards Christian maturity. In this regular program participants are taught the truths of Scripture and doctrine. Some of these people will require much patience as they move towards enrolment as Salvationists. They remember gratefully her personal help and care. Thus her unique ministry complements the work of the corps officer.

General Eva's exemplary life is a living inspiration for every Salvationist. If he were here, the first General of The Salvation Army would be most happy to receive her personal written return of what she is doing 'for God and her fellow men'.

May God grant to us all the necessary wisdom, enthusiasm and strength to join with her and continue this sacred calling in whatever form it may take.

DR BRAMWELL SOUTHWELL, of Australia, served as corps sergeant-major from 1983 until 2007. As a qualified medical practitioner, for 10 years he worked in hospitals in Australia and India. From 1967 until 2005 he was a member of a family medical practice in Melbourne. Since retirement he serves on the board of a non-government community health organisation. He leads a weekly men's Bible study group, and convenes a bi-monthly breakfast meeting and a book discussion group. As CSM he met regularly with the corps officers and ministry team leaders relating to pastoral care, evangelism, discipling, property, and financial stewardship. He commenced a worship program in aged care homes, and served as a lecturer to cadets. His maxim: 'We provide the willingness, God provides the power.' In 1959 he married Margaret Burrows, sister of General Eva Burrows.

12

EDUCATION

COLONEL MARGARET HAY

Out of Fortitude Valley Corps you sprang, Eva, or Eve as you were always called by the small but godly company of women officer teachers who had served with you in Southern Rhodesia in the 1950s and '60s. From them I, a lieutenant and mother juggling calling and kids at Chikankata Secondary School, Zambia, heard stories of you: Eva, the beautiful and bold, in my imagination the Old Testament Eve, Queen Elizabeth I and Catherine Booth morphed into one.

Arriving aged 23 at Howard Institute in the then Southern Rhodesia, you were for the next 22 years to expend your enormous gifts of energy, eloquence and expectancy as an Army educator: for 17 years in Zimbabwe, and from 1970–75 at the International College for Officers in London, then wide-ranging territorial leadership, and finally responsibility for the entire Salvation Army.

The history of the Army's global educational enterprise, with Southern Rhodesia in the mid-20th century as its centrepiece, is so far unwritten, though the latest statistics in *The Salvation Army Year Book* (2009) show that the scope of that enterprise remains impressive. There are over 500,000 students in Army education programs worldwide, ranging from 731 kindergartens, over 1,000 primary schools, 193 secondary schools, 128 vocational training centres and 11 colleges and universities.

While we await the writing of the history, there are plenty of voices in the wind, a sampling of which are heard here from five Army women, strangers to each other and scattered, but comrades in the global salvaging work of education in which you were and are a role model to reckon with. The five are:

Dr Helen Cameron is director of the Oxford Centre for Ecclesiology and Practical Theology and co-chair of the British and Irish Association for Practical Theology. Helen is a soldier of the Oxford Corps, UK.

Major Martha Morales, PTG, was until 2009 training and finance officer at the College for Officer Training in the South America West Territory.

Miss Belindah Munatsi is a qualified electrician, educated in Zimbabwe and currently living in New Zealand. Belindah joined The Salvation Army a decade ago in her home country and is now a soldier in the Upper Hutt Corps, New Zealand.

Ng Man Yee (Margery) is a teacher and chair of the Chinese Department at the William Booth Secondary School, Hong Kong, and a long-standing soldier of the Tai Hang Tung Corps.

Lieut-Colonel Kamla Parshad is principal of the Senior Secondary School and the Catherine Booth College for Girls (the first degree-granting Salvation Army college in India), Batala, India Northern Territory.

Each of the women was asked about early Salvation Army influences on them, about their present work, and their global view of Army educational opportunities and challenges through the lens of the UN Millennium Development Goals. A dominant theme in the testimony of the five about early influences was that, 'the family plays a central role in passing on the faith'. This is illustrated by Kamla recalling that she was 'born and brought up in a Salvation Army family. My parents were officers and my father used to teach village boys and girls in the evening. As I watched him dealing with them very calmly, a vision stirred in me'.

A world away in Peru, Martha, also the child of officers, remembers: 'Our home was always open to anyone who needed to be listened to, encouraged and strengthened. In such an environment I learned to love the Lord and to discover the joy of serving others in varied circumstances. The example of pure values and mutual support were part of my formation and prepared me to serve with joy in varied cultures and lands.'

The testimony of the five also illustrates the potential and potency of the corps as an educational environment. Helen writes: 'Taking part in Army activities as a child and teenager was an education in Bible, music and practical Christianity. Rather like a marinade, my total immersion has left a flavour to my adult life which is inescapable. The Bible and Song Book are the twin pillars of my spirituality—verses come to me unbidden as a commentary on my life.'

On the other hand, Margery, from a non-Christian background, came to faith at the William Booth Secondary School which was closely integrated with the work of the local corps. 'Before studying in William Booth Secondary School (WBSS) I attended a Buddhist primary school. The time at WBSS gave me an opportunity to have contact with the Christian faith. I joined the school choir, gave my life to Jesus, and joined the students' fellowship. I was able to grow spiritually, paving the way for me to become a soldier and finally to meet my future husband.'

Belindah, from a Methodist family, at 17 started being serious about faith and committed herself as a Salvationist. 'My corps officers in Harare were extremely influential in helping me to make these decisions. As well as the Sunday worship, the Wednesday night soldiers' meetings where multi-participation was the norm were a vital part of my Christian education. The officers encouraged us to sing, lead, host the meeting at home and even to teach and preach, giving me on-the-job training in interactive Christian discipleship.'

The five women in the survey were asked what needs and difficulties they see, from the perspective of their present work, for education through the Army. Belindah commented that, though 'equality of opportunity has been quite a strong feature of education in Zimbabwe, when times are hard and resources scarce, it is the girls who suffer. If there is a choice, the boy goes to school'. Martha, from the Latin American perspective concurred, saying: 'Our schools should channel equal opportunities for girls and boys, especially in the countries where strong "machismo" ignores women's and girls' potential.'

Kamla in India sees education as a priority 'with the 1,300 students in my school, to know the students, to teach them the way of salvation, to serve them with heart and soul, to pray for and with them, to visit their homes, and to know the people in society here'. Margery stresses that 'the Army in Hong Kong needs to have professionals to lead our education ministry on a long-term basis in order to introduce and sustain long-lasting strategies for change, with the emphasis always being on moulding our students to be better and more useful in the community and the Kingdom of God'.

Helen describes her main involvement in education in The Salvation

Army as 'encouraging officers to fulfil their educational potential for God's sake. A lifelong ministry needs to be sustained by regular trips to the well of learning—not in search of status—but in search of practical wisdom'.

Looking to the future, the five were asked what role the Army could have in helping to achieve those UN Millennium Development Goals targeting universal primary education and the promotion of gender equality. Helen sees 'the MDGs as a superb vehicle for our conversation in a global Army. Where the Army is a direct provider of school and college education it should aim for the highest standards irrespective of gender, economic or social status. Where the Army is in countries with universal education, it should look for those who need a second chance and develop in them the confidence to learn'.

Belindah agrees, commenting that 'The Salvation Army has high standing in education in Zimbabwe as well as a lot of sway in rural areas'. Martha, with a passion for community engagement, says: 'Latin America is a young continent where the Salvation Army can have a strong influence in breaking barriers and prejudices by means of our varied education centres being really integrated with the people around us'.

And Kamla pulls no punches: 'The Army could open more primary schools to help achieve the goal to provide education for all children, and forge ahead in higher education. To achieve this, the Army should:
• chalk out clear-cut policies to achieve this goal of universal primary education;
• approach UNESCO directly for liberal grants for basic infrastructure facilities;
• create a separate wing at International Headquarters to look after educational activities throughout the world, and expand our higher education activity.'

General Eva is seen by a host of comrades worldwide as the quintessential Salvationist. How apt, hearing the testimonies and challenges in this festschrift paper, that you gave the cream of your service to the educational work of the Army in Zimbabwe and at the ICO. Your first 80 years, along with these testimonies, call forth a hearty 'Hallelujah!' for formation and faith, for gifts, grace and gumption, nurtured in family, corps and school.

But this is not a good old girls' network—these voices, bringing together local and global achievements and concerns, signal also the understanding that our scope is boundless and that no life should be squandered. They urge us, in the light of our Salvationist convictions and the UN Millennium Goals, to be a learning community, to continue to mobilise our precious resources to deliver goals at grassroots level, to value the clear and forceful ideas of serious, systematic thinkers linked to the back streets, and to make the difference that only we can make.

COLONEL MARGARET HAY in 1984 was appointed education officer of The Salvation Army training college in Hong Kong. She also held appointments for six years in the New Zealand training college, including two years as principal. In 1996 she was appointed to positions at International Headquarters in London before taking up a post as Salvation Army visiting minister to Rochester Prison, also holding the responsibility of foreign nationals coordinator. In 2000 she was awarded the London *Times* 'Preacher of the Year', the first woman to win this accolade. From 2001 to 2004 she was principal of The Salvation Army International College for Officers in London and held an International Headquarters special services appointment until her retirement in 2006.

13

VISION

GENERAL PAUL A. RADER (RTD)

The Salvation Army was born of a vision. First, an idea germinating in the heart of God. Then, a living flame in the heart of a man and a woman, William and Catherine Booth. Then, a compelling vision claiming the devotion of a growing Army of Salvation spreading across the world.

It was a vision that found its voice in the captivating imagery of the Founder's vision. Speaking to Staff Officers in Council following the 1904 International Congress (international, for the Army flag was already billowing in 49 countries), he shared his vision of the future. The language is colorful, eloquent, gripping. To have been there would have been to be captivated by the urgent authority of his unmistakable voice, the intensity of his delivery, the very sight of the aging prophet. But more, who could not be mastered by the grandness of the vision he described? 'Having eyes, shall I not see? And having ears, shall I not hear? And having an understanding, shall I not understand? And what I see and hear and understand, shall I not tell to you?

'I see a conflict—a fight—no! More than a fight—a long-continued war... I see again a vast multitude of the miserable, the lonely, the outcasts of Earth . . . the cry of whose agony has come up to Heaven. And I see everywhere among them the mighty blessings conferred upon them by our social operations. I look, and there rises up before my eyes the mightiest and most practical body of Salvation missionaries as yet known upon the Earth. Not less than 100,000 officers, men and women, of all nations, races and tongues, whose business it is to make Salvation known.'

The whole of the vision must be read to understand fully the grip it had on the Founder's heart and imagination and the measure of its impact on his hearers. It was the 'heavenly vision' that impelled and guided the forward march of the flourishing movement.

The Founder's vision was a Kingdom vision. It would have pleased his

Master, for Jesus' vision was a vision of the Kingdom come, for which he taught his disciples and us still to pray.

The Apostle Paul lived and laboured in the grip of a 'heavenly vision' that ever commanded his obedience in mission. It was a vision for the evangelisation of the Gentile nations. The vision produced in him a holy restlessness to reach the 'regions beyond'. It determined his priorities, it energised his questing for souls. It made every hardship, every danger, even the threat of death but 'light and momentary troubles…achieving for us an eternal glory that far outweighs them all' (2 Corinthians 4:17). 'So we fix our eyes not on what is seen, but on what is unseen, since what is seen is temporary, but what is unseen is eternal' (v.18). Indeed, Paul's vision was even grander, for it looked to a day when all God has purposed in Christ will be 'put into effect to bring unity to all things in heaven and on earth under Christ' (Ephesians 1:9–10).

'God has a dream,' writes the redoubtable Archbishop Desmond Tutu in the title of his book subtitled 'A Vision of Hope for our Time'. He was not alone in his stubborn faith that God's vision was for a united and reconciled humanity and the abandonment of the system of bigotry and abuse that had so long divided his nation. It was a vision that endured the long years of struggle against apartheid. It was a vision of hope that the privations and humiliations of the years on Robben Island could not extinguish in the heart of Nelson Mandela during his 'Long Walk to Freedom'. It was the vision that transformed one who should have emerged from his ordeal set on violent revenge into an agent of reconciliation and symbol of hope for the whole divided world.

Crafting a vision may be the project of a team. Capturing vision may be more of an epiphany to a single person. David Yonggi Cho believes he was captured by his vision to lead the largest single congregation in the world. 'I became pregnant with my vision!' But there was a long period of gestation. 'I nurtured the vision. It grew within me…I thought about that "baby" to be "born". I made plans and preparations for it.' 'When the day for the birthing of the vision came,' comments Ted Engstrom, 'Cho was ready for it, and the church was born.' Like an infant, the Full Gospel Church of Yoido in Seoul, Korea began to grow and is growing still. The vision has become a reality.

More often, capturing a vision that resonates with those who must translate it into reality begins with a clear grasp of the context and calling of the organisation. The Founder carefully reviewed the present status and progress of the Army before unveiling his vision. General Eva Burrows understood the historic significance of the demise of the Soviet Union for Christian mission. A door of opportunity for the return of the Army to Russia had been flung open. She recognised it as God's moment. To enter that door required claiming and then casting a compelling vision of possibility. The vision gave impetus to bold and timely action. Eighteen years on, a vital and growing Army in Eastern Europe is the realisation of that vision.

William Booth, ever the sanctified pragmatist, followed his moving oration on his vision for the future of the Army with down-to-earth lectures on good governance, discipline, discharging one's duties and managing the Army's resources.

As Max dePree observes of vision in the corporate setting, fragility is part of the nature of vision. There are no guarantees. The vision must be widely shared and translated into what Donald McGavran used to call 'hard, bold plans'. A compelling vision will have about it a measure of risk, the promise of change and a touch of the unattainable. Not everyone will welcome a disruption of the status quo. Some will resent the moving of the goalposts. The visionary leader with his or her team will be required to live the vision—to celebrate it, to clarify it, to affirm and reaffirm it, and to align policy and practice with it, if it is to maintain its motive power.

In 1975 the Army in Korea had flatlined. Worse, one could extrapolate trends to its inevitable demise. A territorial church growth strategy symposium was convened in November 1976. It included key officers and local officers. As the group assembled, the mood was depressingly negative. Participants first needed to voice their frustration and discouragement. Other churches were thriving. Reasons why they could and the Army could not were rehearsed by one after the other. After two days of intense discussion and prayer, the field secretary, Colonel Kim Soon-bae, declared, 'We can, if we will!' *Hamyun twenda!* The mood changed dramatically. Prayer was the catalyst. The Spirit of God moved on the meeting. The situation had not changed but the perspective had been transformed. Meeting in divisional caucuses, possibilities for new corps plants were discovered. In the end, scores of red markers were placed on a large map of South Korea indicating communities without a corps where a plant might be possible. Then someone called for a map of North Korea. One was hastily sketched and attached to the map of the South. Soon, it too was dotted with markers. In a final unforgettable moment of commitment, the territorial commander, Commissioner Chun Yong-sup, led in prayer while all the participants placed a hand on the map, claiming the vision for their own.

In 2008 the territory celebrated its centenary in magnificent congress events led by General Shaw Clifton and Commissioner Helen Clifton supported by the territorial leaders, Commissioners Chun Kwang-pyo and Yu Sung-ja. Thousands of Salvationists gathered in Seoul to celebrate God's blessing on the vision, so much of which had been realised. But a fresh vision has now captured the spiritual imagination of Korean Salvationists. The congress web site included video segments that colourfully visualised the Army in Korea in 2028 as a centre of global mission. The vision was introduced in the World Missions Rally during the congress. It was expressed in a vision and mission statement for the centenary and beyond. The statement called for renewal and growth at home (Jerusalem), expanded services in the society (Judea) and a mission of reconciliation and compassion in the North (Samaria). The vision anticipates 1,000 more corps in a reunified Korea, 1,004 more officers and 1,004 youth and lay workers, while sending out 100 workers for overseas ministries by the year 2028 (the ends of the Earth).

Overly ambitious? Perhaps. If God owns the vision, nothing is impossible. The vision God will bless issues from his heart. As veteran missionary to Korea, David Ross, observes, 'Only those who know God's heart are invited to know his plan for his people'. If so, then the urgent cry for visionary leadership in our time must first be for us all a serious call to intimacy with God.

GENERAL PAUL A. RADER (Rtd) was in 1994 the first American-born officer to be elected General. He had earned BA, BD and M Th. Degrees, and a Doctor of Missiology and several honorary degrees. Upon commissioning the Raders were appointed to Korea, where they served as missionaries for the next 22 years, both becoming proficient in the Korean language. His final appointment in Korea was as chief secretary. In the USA he served as training principal, divisional commander, chief secretary and territorial commander. He is a Paul Harris Fellow of Rotary, and President Kim Dae-jung of the Republic of Korea awarded him the Order of Diplomatic Service Merit in 1998. Following retirement in 1999 Dr Rader was elected to the presidency of his alma mater, Asbury College, from 2000 to 2006. The Raders' life story is told in *If Two Shall Agree*, by Carroll Hunt Rader.

14

P R A Y E R

L Y N D A L L   B Y W A T E R

'Who is God then?' The question came from one of the 10 teenagers who had just descended on The Salvation Army building in Burnley, England. The evening meeting was in full swing, but the act of worship proved too restrictive an environment for the fascinated and over-excited young people. So two members of the congregation took them next door for refreshments. As they drank and chatted, questions flowed thick and fast, and so did the gospel.

The corps in question did not have a particularly thriving ministry among the young people of the local community. Teenagers had been 'hanging around' outside the building for a while, but they had never shown much interest in crossing the threshold. What made that night so different? Very simply the fact that Burnley Corps had decided to do a week of 24-7 non-stop prayer. The sign outside their building advertised the fact, and the teenagers had come in response to that sign. They wanted to know about prayer.

They say you should be careful what you ask for, and this is perhaps more true in prayer than in anything else. Those 10 teenagers returned day after day, messing up the beautifully ordered prayer room with their liveliness and their creativity and, at the end of the week, a small youth group had formed. I have no doubt that the congregation had been looking forward to a week of peaceful, contemplative encounters with God, but instead they got a week of welcoming the confused and the hurting; a week of allowing their 'prayer closet' to be invaded by the very people for whom they were praying.

Throughout its history, The Salvation Army has proven to be a band of men and women who cannot separate prayer from mission, or mission from prayer. From its earliest days its leaders and soldiers have known that there is only one war to fight: the war against Satan's schemes to destroy.

The weapons may vary—food to combat hunger, forgiveness to wash away shame, praise to banish spiritual darkness—but all these have simply been seen as different aspects of the same war. Consequently, wherever the seeds of Salvation Army work have flourished, we find that the fibres of prayer, mission and social justice are irrevocably intertwined.

From time to time, the Lord shows us that certain individual fibres need strengthening, if the three are to continue thriving together. During General Eva Burrows' tenure as head of this global family, she presided over various initiatives to powerfully strengthen the fibre of mission and church growth. Since then, we have seen an explosion of renewed energy for spreading the good news of the gospel of Jesus Christ in a whole host of creative and culturally accessible ways. In recent years, leaders both at international and territorial level have observed that the fibre of prayer is growing weaker, and so have appointed leaders with the task of strengthening that particular aspect of the Army's life and work. As one of those leaders, I am delighted to say that it is often difficult to tease out the prayer fibre, because it is so deeply bound up with our passion for reaching a dying world. My prayer is that we will never become good at 'stand-alone prayer'!

This intertwining of prayer, mission and social justice serves to keep the prayer life of a Salvationist blessedly simple and selfless. We are trained to know who we are in Christ—to contentedly accept the truth that we are sinners saved by grace (Ephesians 2:8–10). Prayer is not a recitation of complicated liturgy, it is a much-needed visit to the Mercy Seat (whether literal or metaphorical), and to receive the fresh grace and peace we need for the tasks that lie ahead of us. What's more, we learn that our lives are not an end in themselves—but that we are called to spend ourselves on behalf of others. Prayer can be an hour spent serving hot coffee to the victims of a disaster, blessing each one as we put the cup in their hands.

Yet, while the prayers we pray may be simple, the goals we aim for are huge. In her closing address to a strategic growth conference General Eva Burrows reminded the delegates of the story of Booth-Tucker, who started the work in India. She told how he travelled there with just three companions, knowing that God had sent him, and believing that, in God, the Army would greatly impact that vast nation. She then went on to say that the number of Salvationists in the five territories of India had by that point risen to over 300,000. (There are now six territories with nearly 330,000 soldiers.)

To be a Salvationist is to believe that transformation is possible. And that kind of faith requires a consistent, disciplined prayer life. We are called to live beyond our means; we are invited to step way beyond what we believe to be possible, so that God can use us to do the impossible. If we want to live that kind of life, we soon discover that we need to be daily tapping into the resources which Jesus has made available for us through his death and resurrection, and that those resources are accessed entirely through prayer.

Scripture is also clear that, if we want to see true transformation in our world, we must have an accurate and confident understanding of the authority we have in Christ. Prayer is not merely the 'filling station' for our personal life and ministry; it is the weapon given to us to dismantle the works of the evil one (2 Corinthians 10:3,4). We need to be active in prayer in the heavenlies, if we are to see thorough transformation on the Earth.

Heartening though this analysis of the Salvationist's prayer life may be, we must not be blind to what we lack. The very simplicity of our approach to prayer has, at times, been our downfall. We have not wanted to over-complicate or over-formulate, and consequently we have sometimes failed to give prayer either the weight of importance or the depth of insight it deserves.

Some years ago, General Burrows was invited to speak at a youth conference in Australia, and was asked to summarise her governing principles. One of them was, quite simply, yet profoundly stated: 'There is no substitute for prayer'.

When prayer intertwines with mission and social justice, it can begin to be eroded by activity. It can become a last resort, rather than the backbone of our Christian lives. This may have been less of a problem for the first Salvationists, living and working as they did in a society which was still largely Christian in its foundational values. But in the 21st century it is a grave danger, particularly in the West, where Christian spirituality is on the decrease.

As I write, I sit just 60 miles or so from where The Salvation Army began, and I reflect that, though poverty and addiction are still real and present problems here, we arguably suffer more from the deadening effects of wealth and consumerism. Our Western societies are desperately in need of churches full of people whose lives are steeped in truth and soaked in the Holy Spirit. It is no longer enough to have 'said our prayers' in the morning. We need to have dug through the silt of apathy and self-contentedness, and to have plunged deep into the refreshing, refocusing presence of God, if we are to carry something truly enriching into the desert places of our society.

My petition, as this book goes forth, is: 'Lord, I pray for your Salvation Army. May we be born in prayer; may we begin in prayer; may we be immersed in prayer. And then, empowered by your Spirit, may we live for the salvation of the world. Amen.'

LYNDALL BYWATER since 2001 has been coordinator for the Army's 24-7 Prayer Network in the UK Territory. The heart of her job is to promote prayer, produce resources with her team for Salvationists to use in their personal prayer lives, help leadership teams develop prayer strategy in their corps, and conduct territorial prayer gatherings and training events. She also works with national prayer organisa-tions, including 24-7 Prayer and the Prayer Forum of the British Isles and Ireland. She writes and teaches on prayer, and loves nothing more than seeing people released into new freedom in their prayer lives. Although without her physical sight, through her ministry on prayer she brings the light of Christ to many. Her heart is to see the Church in her nation find a new thirst for God, and a new depth in its walk with him.

15

DOCTRINE

COMMISSIONER WILLIAM FRANCIS

Renowned British author, educator and lay Anglican theologian Dorothy Sayers (1893–1957) produced a popular series of 12 radio dramas entitled *The Man Born to be King*. Each episode depicted an epoch of Jesus' life, from the events surrounding his birth to his death and resurrection. The BBC broadcast the play cycle throughout war-torn Britain on Sunday evenings, with the monthly episodes commencing in December 1941.

Prior to the debut performance, a reporter asked Dorothy Sayers, 'What do you hope to teach through these plays?' Without hesitation she replied, 'Doctrine!' After an awkward pause, the journalist probed, 'Doctrine? Won't that be boring?' 'Indeed not,' Dr. Sayers answered— 'Doctrine is the drama!'

OUR HISTORIC HALLMARK

In general, doctrine designates the teaching (religious or political) of any group or individual. Doctrine is a principle, or a body of such principles, that serves as the foundation for the group or person's mission.

The Greek word is *didaskalia*, meaning teaching, instruction. This word is used 21 times in the New Testament. A companion word, *didaxe* (also meaning teaching), is used 30 times. Including all forms, the total use of this idea of doctrine numbers 207 in the New Testament. This is a noteworthy recurrence of the root for a biblical concept.

Christian doctrine has three fundamental and indispensable characteristics. It is *theological*. The word 'theology' stems from two Greek words—*theos*, meaning God and *logos* meaning reason. Together they form the concept of a 'reasoned discourse about God'. Doctrine is therefore sound, articulate, reasoned dialogue about God.

Christian doctrine is also *ethical*. It addresses human behaviour and conduct. What we believe becomes the foundation for how we live.

Christian doctrine is ultimately *biblical,* based on the Bible. In the salient words of the Army's Founder, William Booth, 'Our creed is the Bible'.

The Salvation Army's doctrine—its theological underpinnings—provides firm support for the drama of its mission. What is believed to be true about the Scriptures, the Triune God, sin, salvation and sanctification, sustains and empowers that mission. Except for the Bible, no other document is more central and indispensable to fulfilling the Army's historic, God-ordained mission than are the fundamental tenets of its 11 points of doctrine.

In order to safeguard and advance The Salvation Army's articles of faith, General Edward Higgins created in 1931 a Doctrine Council at International Headquarters. Its duties were 'to examine and report to the General as to the correctness and harmony with Salvation Army principles and doctrines, as defined in the Deed Poll of 1878, of the teaching contained in all Salvation Army publications such as song books, company orders, directories, advanced training, and similar lesson courses and text books, and other publications in which doctrinal teaching appears in any form'.

While the International Doctrine Council continues to fulfil its historic mandate and responsibilities, General Eva Burrows and subsequent international leaders have augmented the council's undertakings. The contemporary council is:

• entrusted to be 'faithful custodians of Army doctrinal positions' including the articles of faith and other positions set down in approved Salvation Army publications and statements;

• asked to recommend ways in which Salvation Army beliefs might be taught more effectively;

• empowered to undertake inter-church dialogues and conversations at the General's direction;

• expected to keep in touch with theological trends internationally, maintaining contacts with relevant institutions and academics both inside and outside The Salvation Army.

In recent years, the council has participated in formal dialogues with other Christian denominations, including the Seventh Day Adventist Church and the World Methodist Council. The WMC serves as an umbrella assembly of 77 separate denominations stemming from the same Wesleyan historical and theological roots. The purpose of these formal gatherings is one of increased mutual understanding through open, collegial dialogue. Bilateral dialogues will not take place if the other denominations view these meetings as leading to ecclesiastical merger, absorption or organic union of any kind. The goal clearly remains that of open theological and ecclesiological dialogue to the end of strengthening friendship, mutual understanding and cooperation in countries where both denominations minister.

PRESENT ASSURANCE — KNOWING THE TRUTH

Throughout the history of the church, followers of Christ have sought assurance that truth can be understood and followed. While with Pilate they have asked the question, 'What is truth?' (John 18:38), Christians have meant something quite different by the question. Pilate's question calls attention to the fact that his encounter with Jesus was much more than the meeting of two individuals. It was the meeting of two cultures— Ancient Greek and Ancient Hebrew. Pilate and Jesus meant something quite different when discussing the word 'truth'.

Our Lord understood truth from an Eastern way of thinking that defined truth in terms of a person and not a proposition; the Hebrew understanding of practical relationship, rather than an objective prop-osition embodied truth for Jesus. In both the Old and New Testaments, truth both describes and defines a person, not a proposition or an idea. In the Hebrew mind, truth is verified by the person who declares it, not by a written or verbal proposition alone.

When Jesus declared to his disciples, 'You will know the truth, and the truth will set you free' (John 8:32), he was not describing a set of propositional truths that if adhered to will bestow freedom. He was describing himself as Truth.

On another occasion Jesus affirmed, 'I am the way and the truth and the life. No-one comes to the Father except through me' (John 14:6). Once again, Jesus underscores that truth is a person. His words are true essentially because he declared them to be true.

We are far more children of ancient Athens than Jerusalem. We better understand Pilate's question than Jesus' answer. Essentially, doctrinal truth originates in a relationship with Christ. He alone provides present assurance. What we believe is developed, confirmed and empowered because of the believer's continued relationship with Christ.

Theology—what we understand and experience about God—invigorates life, motivates conduct, moulds the spirit, purifies the nature, and solidifies the believer's relationship with God, with others and with oneself. Believers strive to daily articulate, promote, resource, teach, proclaim and participate in the divine drama. In the words of Peter, 'In your hearts set apart Christ as Lord. Always be prepared to give an answer to everyone who asks you to give the reason for the hope that you have. But do this with gentleness and respect' (1 Peter 3:15). Peter challenges us to understand, live and proclaim what we believe.

Understanding and living doctrine is as indispensable for the individual as it is for a denomination. As a devoted disciple seeking truth, the Salvationist arrives at theological positions through reading God's written revelation, the Scriptures. Doctrinal truths are processed and confirmed through dialogue with other Christians via witness, sermons and direct instruction, as well as through the writings of others. Essentially, however, theological discernment results from the believer's personal relationship with Christ and the teaching of the Holy Spirit. Jesus has not left us without a Teacher. 'But the Counsellor,' Jesus promised, 'the Holy Spirit, whom the Father will send in my name, will teach you all things and will remind you of everything I have said to you' (John 14:26).

Towards the end of his remarkable life, the well-known evangelist and founder of Methodism, John Wesley, expressed his concern for the future of Methodism. His words provide a persistent warning to his ecclesiastical cousins, The Salvation Army. 'I am not afraid,' John Wesley asserts, 'that the people called Methodists should ever cease to exist either in Europe or America. But I am afraid lest they should only exist as a dead sect, having the form of religion without the power. And this undoubtedly will be the case unless they hold fast both the doctrine, spirit, and discipline with which they first set out.' Let us take heed and heart from these words of challenge.

COMMISSIONER WILLIAM W. FRANCIS is territorial commander for the Canada and Bermuda Territory. He earned a master of divinity degree, received an honorary doctoral degree and is chancellor of the landmark Booth College campus in Canada. Since 2006 he has served as chairman of the International Doctrine Council. Earlier appointments included, with his wife Marilyn, serving as corps officer, divisional leader, territorial youth secretary, training principal, personnel secretary, chief secretary and international secretary for the Americas. An effective exponent of the Word, he is author of *The Stones Cry Out*, and *Celebrate the Feasts of the Lord*.

16

LITERATURE

COMMISSIONER WESLEY HARRIS

From the beginning of The Salvation Army there has been a constant flow of writings that have defined us and helped us to fulfil our mission in the world. Salvationists have produced a vast number of songs and poems, articles and books—munitions for an army in the field engaged in a war against the forces of evil.

William and Catherine Booth, our Founders, were prime examples. Though they lived incredibly busy lives and were under immense pressure as they sought to lead God's army into battle, they grasped every available moment to put pen to paper for the furtherance of the gospel.

When I was a young Salvation Army officer my mentor was retired Commissioner George Jolliffe who as young private secretary to William Booth actually lived in his home. He told me that sometimes in the dead of night he would hear a little bell tinkling in the Founder's bed-room while a commanding voice called, 'Jolliffe, I can't sleep, let's work!' Whereupon young Jolliffe, in his night attire no doubt, would go, notebook in hand, to help his octogenarian general capture some fleeting inspiration for an article.

From 1865 and the beginnings of what became The Christian Mission and later The Salvation Army until the end of his life in 1912, William Booth's literary output was prodigious, with few weeks failing to yield up material from his fiery pen. What is more, there is little doubt that he encouraged—even commanded—others to do likewise!

Catherine was also a prolific writer. Frail in health, the mother of eight children, and with a diary packed with speaking engagements, nonetheless found time to write articles both lucid and immensely challenging. Like her husband she knew how to use the weapon of words—written or spoken—and being dead she still speaks!

With Salvation Army literature it has never been a case of 'art for art's sake'. General Eva Burrows commended writing that clarified the vision of The Salvation Army in the minds of those who read it. That meant that essentially our literature should be about Jesus Christ and what he has done and can do in the lives of those who accept him. That was the focus from the beginning. As editor of *The War Cry* published in London I was thrilled to receive reports of people being converted as a result of reading that paper sometimes described as 'the white-winged messenger'.

Early writers like Bramwell Booth, George S. Railton and Frederick Booth-Tucker not only delighted in recording the exploits of early-day salvation warriors but in proclaiming how the doctrine of holiness was exemplified in their lives. What counted was not just what they *did* but what they *were* with God's help. Ungodly people were transfigured by grace while still remaining very human, and their example was highlighted by our writers so that others might see their good works and glorify their Father in heaven.

An outstanding early-day writer was Samuel Brengle—the first American to become a commissioner in the Army, revered for his teaching of the Wesleyan doctrine of holiness and for the saintliness of his personal life. He wrote many books on holiness and these have had, and continue to have, a wide influence in many parts of the Church universal.

A graceful writer and scholarly exponent of the doctrine of holiness was Frederick Coutts. His early officership was spent in corps work and then for 18 years he served in the Army's International Literary Department where his responsibilities included the compilation of the lessons for Army's Sunday schools throughout the world. Later, leadership of the Army in the Eastern Territory of Australia preceded his election as General which position he held from 1963 to 1969. In retirement his extensive writing included volumes six and seven of *The History of the Salvation Army.*

The compiler of this volume, Colonel Henry Gariepy, OF, should also be recognised for the current, unparalleled circulation of his books outside as well as within the Army. Along with innumerable articles, his 30 published volumes have gained wide acceptance. They have been mainly on biblical and devotional topics but also include the official biography of General Eva Burrows and volume eight of *The History of*

The Salvation Army. Happily, he continues to write!

A chapter about the heritage of Army literature must include reference to its richest vein, the words of songs. Without doubt the most memorable writings of Salvationists are those that have been set to music. From the beginning we were a singing Army and learnt a lot of our theology through singing about it.

Many of our early-day songs were set to secular tunes, before copyright restrictions were as stringent as they are today. Granted, some of the lyrics had little literary merit but they still had an appeal and soul-saving messages which went to the hearts of the people who crowded Army buildings. Many songs fell into disuse but others had an enduring quality and remain.

One of the most notable of Army songwriters was Albert Orsborn who became the sixth General of the Army. As a young officer he was on the staff of the officer training college in London at the time when up to 3,000 attended the weekly holiness meetings in the Clapton Congress Hall. He was instructed by the college principal to write words for a new song every week, often set to one of the pop tunes of the day. Incredibly, some of his offerings are still sung around the Army world to this day.

Similarly, pressure produced inspiration in the 1960s and '70s when two young officer-friends of mine (who both became Generals in the Army) were asked to produce religious musicals that played to huge crowds around the world. At one stage John Larsson and I were working at the Army's headquarters in Glasgow and John Gowans was stationed in Manchester. The latter would phone words that might be scribbled on the back of an envelope and shortly afterwards the music would be composed on the piano below my office. Some of the verses written in such ways have become known around the world.

Many of those who have contributed to our literary heritage would want to pay tribute to those who encouraged them to begin and continue to write for God and the Army, sometimes through arranging suitable training. I, for one, valued the encouragement of people such as Lieut-Commissioner Arch R. Wiggins and Commissioner Reginald Woods who not only courteously acknowledged the submissions of a youthful lieutenant but gave encouragement without which my efforts at writing might have ceased soon after they began.

NOT ONLY WRITERS

In this chapter about the Army's literary heritage tribute has been paid to authors, but what of others who have often made their work acceptable and available? When the last word of a book or article has been written that may not be the end but only the beginning of its effective life.

What of the editors labouring behind the scenes to eliminate factual and grammatical errors? What of others in an editorial team who make pages inviting and readable even for those without 20/20 vision? (Poor layout and typography can make even the most gripping narrative seem boring and off-putting.)

Thanks are also due to those who market and distribute Army literature. The large circulation of some of our periodicals around the world may owe much to those who faithfully take them to taverns and street corners in the name of the Lord. The standing and status of such literature evangelism deserves recognition.

It is heartening that with the encouragement of General Shaw Clifton, himself an able scholar and author, there has been increased emphasis on the production of new books in many countries, and also the reprinting of Army classics.

On the understanding that if we do not innovate we will enervate, some volumes may now be downloaded from the internet or taped, particularly for the sight-impaired. So what next?

There is a bright future for Army literature. Aided by modern means of production and communication it can be full of promise. Just as a couple of decades ago, under the inspired leadership of General Burrows, the Army saw a window of opportunity and moved into areas previously barred against us, such as in Eastern Europe, so new printing techniques and electronic means now available can open up opportunities to take our message to more people in many more places. Let us honour our heritage by accepting the challenge of the future!

COMMISSIONER WESLEY HARRIS for over 25 years ministered at Army corps in Britain, including Regent Hall, the only church in London's famous Oxford Street, where the spectrum of ministry ranged from pavement to palace and links with the homeless and the royal family. Service followed in Scotland and Australia, and  at the 1986 High Council he set a precedent as a candidate for General, with the rank of colonel. His final appointment was to leadership of the Canada and Bermuda Territory. Before training for officership he was engaged in journalism and became one of the Army's foremost literary contributors, having served as editor-in-chief at IHQ, and with an aggregate of some 70,000 copies of his nine books in print, the latest entitled *Dear Paul*.

17

MUSIC AND THE ARTS

COLONELS GWENYTH AND ROBERT REDHEAD

Here is a story of two tents. In June 2004, the 2nd International Music and other Creative Arts Forum (MOSAIC) was held in Canada. It was attended by 61 delegates from 34 territories and commands, one-half representing the developing world. The forum sought to increase the effectiveness of the worldwide Salvation Army in its approach to worship and evangelism. On the fourth of the five-day conference, 900 friends from the Toronto area were welcomed to enjoy an open-air barbecue with the delegates, and then to share in worship in a large tent. The scene in the grounds of the Jackson's Point Conference Center was beautiful, a perfect place in which to worship God.

One hundred and forty years earlier in another large tent, William Booth also worshipped. The decor was not as affluent, and the scenery in East London left much to be desired. The worship was rowdy, basic in its style, yet both congregations shared a common ideal—a desire to connect with God.

In its early formative days the Army was very much a product of its time. We quote Lieut-Colonel Max Ryan: 'The Army made a lasting impact upon its cultural environment because it took some of the important features of secular culture, sanctified them and used them as instruments for the advancement of God's Kingdom. Examples include brass bands and music hall tunes, open-air meetings, a revivalist approach to religion, use of public buildings for meetings. These beginnings were marked by innovation, not strategically designed, but as passionate responses to clearly perceived needs.'

The later tent also revealed a response to this challenge, now as a 19th century movement adapting to the postmodern world. The endeavours first commandeered whatever accessible music and arts that might aid the message, such as drama (even preaching from a coffin!), music (voice, strings, reeds and, eventually virtually exclusively, brass), whereas the second used the whole gamut of modern music, drama, dance, multi-media, etc.

Both tents were a response to 'uncharted' waters. The first, with little concept of where it may lead; the second, with a strategic view to moving the worldwide Army to reach out in new ways as a means of reaching a population which saw little relevance or value in 'traditional religion'.

There were also some major differences. Any movement that is so uniquely in tune with the age in which it is born is most likely to face challenges of identity in its second century. That first world exemplified empire, militarism, religious fervour, with church-going being the norm, and a class system that was perceived as deemed by decree! The second revealed a world of individualism, both at national and local level, where there are no 'absolutes', and people create their own 'gods'.

So why in these days do we use the phrase 'music and the arts'? Surely music is an 'art-form' too! The title in the Army has been instituted more recently as a result of the inclusion in our worship of various creative styles which have crept in from other churches. In older days, evangelicalism in general was suspicious of the use of the 'arts'. In the Army, our territorial departments were often called band and songster departments, and a summer music school 'band' camp, which highlights the historic centrality for so long of the band and songsters (and youth equivalents) in our worship and evangelism. Music was central and any other 'art form' was very much on the periphery.

In this new age we see bands and songsters generally no longer central, particularly in the developed world, and many corps emulating the music styles of other churches. The sad aspect is not that we are changing from our cherished forms to meet the present-day challenges, but that we have become followers of trends rather than the innovative leaders of change as we were in our formative days.

Looking back at the beginning of brass and vocal predominance, our first band—the Fry Family (father and three adult sons)—brought their brass quartet to the open-air meeting in Salisbury, England in 1878, primarily to help protect the women Salvationists from the marauding mob. However, their 'brass band' took off and, although our Founder was initially dubious about the number of bands growing up all around, it was obvious they were enabling us to connect with the populace. The development of songster brigades did not come until later, partly because of the Founder's concern not to develop 'music for music's sake' (as he had perceived in many church choirs).

One of the Army's 'statesmen' in this early development was Richard Slater, affectionately known as 'the father of Salvation Army music'. With his skill as a well-trained classical musician, his recognition of the power of music in relating to people, and his big vision for a worldwide development of music in the Army, he founded a music department which exemplified two remarkable concepts in terms of making music—that every Salvationist should have the opportunity to make a contribution, and the music was always to be for the glory of God. These became hallmarks of the Army's 'free giving of service for the Lord' that created high standards of commitment in all musicians. The department received, vetted and produced songs, band arrangements and accompaniments, and over the years, now with similar departments in many territories, has produced some of the finest 'religious' musicians with a repertoire of music which is the envy of many.

Around the end of the Army's first century, a quite remarkable artistic development took place—the birth of the Joystrings; not a strategically designed program, but a response to a spontaneous comment by the then new General in response to a newspaper reporter's question of whether The Salvation Army was going to start using guitars. The Beatles were creating an appetite in the masses for a completely different style of music. The Church universal at that time was still generally locked into the organ as the accompaniment for song worship. Thus the Army had the opportunity to lead much of Christendom, particularly the evangelicals, into a whole new approach to worship and evangelism, reaching the masses with a relevant gospel as we did in our beginnings.

Sadly, we were unable to seize the moment. Probably the fear of endangering the strong institution of the traditional musical sound of the Army clouded our vision and we failed to grasp the opportunity given us. Very soon this musical style was viewed as the domain of 'just the young people'.

Thankfully, in recent years, there has been a widening of the scope of the Army's expression in worship and evangelism. The need to relate an intelligible gospel to this age requires a relevant language, and the arts (including music) is one of the vehicles most suited to succeeding. The secret is to develop a good understanding of the meaning of worship. It is not about worship styles; it is about a relationship with God, responding to his revelation of himself to us. The arts often express what the heart cannot put into words, and we believe that all our talents are to be used for the Lord and his kingdom. We have been marvellous, worldwide, at expressing it through music, but what of our gifted actors, dancers, artists? In many places, the regular Sunday worship reveals the same uncreative form week by week, ignoring the artistic abilities that could enhance the message so effectively.

The era in which we are now living has been variously described as postmodern, multi-sensory and digital. Unfortunately, the inclusion of the arts (including music) in worship is still perceived in many places as an 'item' or 'special feature', rather than a facet of worship. Why then did God give some of our people such fine artistic gifts? He doesn't want just another 'item' that gives a little more colour to the meeting. He wants to hear the heart of the artist expressing a particular truth that can best be realised by the congregation through the arts—for them to feel the power of the message as well as hearing it.

This also shows that there is still a place for the substantive music works of some of our greatest composers, such as Eric Ball, Ray Steadman-Allen and Kenneth Downie. We need to be creative in helping our congregations who have increasingly become used to the three-minute sound bite attention span, to experience in-depth listening which can reach their hearts. This is where the judicious use of multimedia can help congregations to engage.

Two of the outcomes of Mosaic were the ratification of international guidelines for worship committees and international principles and guidelines for gospel arts groups. The means for change are in place, but as yet have not been widely embraced. All we need is the faith and courage to recognise it and be willing to invest ourselves to be more creative in our worship. There is much positive creativity happening all around The

Salvation Army world. Let us encourage it and allow it to blossom, so that the worship that takes place in any Salvation Army setting can incorporate the best artistic expressions to support the message being proclaimed so that the end result will be transformational.

COLONELS ROBERT AND GWENYTH REDHEAD served in corps, the training college, international music editorial department, and later in New Zealand and Canada. Robert served as territorial music secretary and bandmaster of the Canadian Staff Band, while Gwenyth became the territory's first drama consultant. Robert's music has been published by the Army around the world, and many of his works have been recorded. From 1990 to 1994 Robert headed the International Music Editorial Department, was bandmaster of International Staff Band, and later directed the creative ministries in the new UK territory. Their

last appointment was the General's representatives for the development of worship and evangelism through music and other creative arts. They retired in Canada in 2005, now rendering worship leadership in their corps. They give testimony that their ministry in music and the arts received both official and personal support and encouragement from General Eva Burrows.

18

MENTORSHIP

MAJOR BEVERLY IVANY

When the CEO of General Electric Co. was asked about the most important lesson he learned from his mentor, he responded: 'The importance of people; attracting them, inspiring them, teaching them, encouraging them, challenging them'. Another executive leader recently said that a mentor is necessary for two reasons: 'to deny you the complacency of a plateau, and to urge you on to the peak of your potential—and beyond'. The *Howard Business Review* goes on to say that people need mentors; mentors who encourage risk-taking, who impart a philosophical commitment to sharing, and who help to develop relationship-building in an intuitive and empathetic manner.

Mentorship is defined as 'a formal relationship between a student and an adult to further the student's knowledge, skills, or career'. I firmly believe, as a child of officer parents, an officer of over 30 years, and a mother of four, that mentorship is a definite hallmark of the Army—for the present, and for the days that lie ahead. For are we not about relationships; being there for one another, to help one another use discernment and wisdom as we are challenged to engage postmodern culture and confront the ever-changing world of tomorrow?

Perhaps some feel mentorship is not really necessary—it is only for the young, weak and inexperienced. True, to be mentored is to be humbled. But humility is a strength; both receiving and giving contributes to spiritual growth and maturity, fully desiring to be like Jesus, and inviting others to do likewise. Imagine what a difference it would make for the future of the Army if all Salvationists embraced this fundamental concept of mentorship.

What then is needed in order to be a good mentor? I suggest five fundamental qualities, five Christian characteristics that could not only form *us*, but potentially help shape The Salvation Army of tomorrow:

Relational Connection: A mentor needs, regardless of age, race, socio-economic status, to be someone who loves people and can connect with them. Jesus loved all. People were drawn to his magnetic personality. He did not discriminate; he practised justice and fairness for all, including the marginalised, the ostracised and the vulnerable.

He then chose twelve to mentor specifically. They had flaws, but they also had tremendous potential. They were human, making many mistakes along the way. But, because of a developing relationship and a strong connection with their mentor, they grew and matured. We, likewise, must care deeply for others.

Weapons of 'mass distraction' exist in our world to so easily take us away from the fundamental essence of relationship-building. As we focus on relationships, our families will become more healthy, and our interpersonal connections will not be forced but will evolve naturally. People are our brothers and sisters—to be treasured and held in high esteem; to be forgiven and then engaged—making for a family-oriented Army, within the Body of Christ.

Intuitive Listening Skills: There is noise all around us, even in our supposed quiet times. We put iPods in our ears to shut out the noise, only to take in a different kind of noise. It's hard to find solitude and silence. True stillness before God is elusive. When we do find quietness, we tend to be uncomfortable with it. We deal with so much 'stuff', so much clutter in our lives. Our instinctive reaction is to talk to God—to get everything out.

Mentors need to be in tune with themselves first; ready to effectively listen to what others are saying, or not saying. Mentors are needed to shed wisdom and insight; to guide, to walk with people and to help them along the journey of life.

Listening is not easy—for our natural tendency is to speak. Mentors must discipline themselves in listening to God's voice, to hear 'the sweet music of his voice', affirming that God's love *is* wonderful.

Listening to him. Listening to others. Being silent. God has so much he wants to teach us, to say to us, to give to us. Are we receptive, willing to be an 'instrument of his peace' for another? This will make for a more sensitive Army.

Trustworthiness: I recently asked a young woman who I was mentoring for the first time, 'What do you expect from this mentoring relationship?' She immediately responded: 'To be able to say everything and anything and to know it will go nowhere else.' God forbid a breach of confidence, even as a 'prayer concern', of those who trust us with the intimacy of their hearts. We may not intend to be malicious, but it can happen through unguarded carelessness.

We all need 'safe places'. We all need people with whom we can share; people we can trust wholeheartedly, people who are trustworthy. One would think this would be a natural for the Church, for the Army. But too often we have not done well with this, officially or personally. But we are dealing with more than governance or hierarchy here.

Let us be people who hold confidences, who are trustworthy. When someone walks through a 'dark night of the soul', may we walk with them, non-judgmentally, but guiding them to the light, as a friend. Yes, God calls us to be an Army of integrity.

Heart: Our motto is 'Heart to God, hand to man'. Sometimes I wish it were 'Heart to God and heart to man'. We must beware of losing heart. Of doing, instead of being. Of helping, but simply going through the motions. We are to love not only the work and ministry, but the individuals, for who they are, in Christ.

I may receive great wisdom and direction from someone, which can help me through a situation—even a crisis. But if there is no heart in it, something is missing. I may be there for someone, and give guidance and insight from my experience as an officer, or from life itself. But if my heart is not in it, something vital is lacking. We do well to remember that 'people don't care how much you know, until they know how much you care'.

Let us not forget that our actions and support are significant. Let us also recognise that our presence is significant as well. The heart is in what I say, and also in what I do not say. This is true *agape* love—Christ, loving through us. Transformation begins with a heart's desire for deeper relationships. Hearts baptised with the fire of the Holy Spirit. Yes, an Army of 'heart', above all else.

Being Spiritually Alive: I could only be attracted to a mentor who is fully alive spiritually. I recently asked a large group of young people what barriers might prevent them from 'signing up' to be officers in the Army. Their immediate response was 'officers'. I was shocked; and then soberly realised that any of us can cast a negative spirit.

One can be spiritually alive for a season and then the spirit of joy can gradually be snuffed out by negativity or discouragement, or even cynicism. We are led to pray, 'Oh, Father in Heaven, may I be fully alive in Christ, so that when people see me, they see something of his reflection in me.'

Have I ever failed in this area? Do I fall short? Of course; more times than I'd ever like to admit. But I long, with God's help, to share my passion for him with others. My constant prayer: 'Radiate thy beauty in me! As you shine, Jesus, shine, in all your majesty, in all your glory, may I in turn shine for you. Make us a radiant Army so as to touch others for your glory.'

MAJOR BEVERLY IVANY with her husband has served in corps, at the training college, and as divisional leaders in Quebec. She has authored two books for young people and numerous published articles. She is an accomplished musician, with a bachelor of music, a bachelor of arts (English), and is currently finishing her masters of theological studies. She has been a guest speaker and teacher at various conferences, and in Toronto was president of Rotary and awarded the Paul Harris Fellowship. She loves to read, write, preach, jog and make music. Her present position is candidates secretary for the Canada and Bermuda Territory.

19

PENTECOST POWER

GENERAL JOHN GOWANS (RTD)

Pentecost should be celebrated by every Christian, whatever their denomination. Ignored by the secular world, Pentecost should be on a par with Christmas as far as Christians are concerned. It's the birthday of the Church and should be marked by a party. Yes, balloons and cakes and flags are well in order.

Pentecost is also a time for prayer—a time to ask God for the transforming power of the Holy Spirit to be made manifest in our life. And having asked for it, receive it! Let's hold out open hands and allow God to do his work in us. If we want it, it's ours! God loves to answer our prayers.

FROM THE BEGINNING

The Holy Spirit was active in our world from the very beginning. There was never a time when he was not in existence and at work. He was there even before the beginning, if we can understand such a concept. When everything we see and everything that exists was just a thought in the mind of God, the Holy Spirit shared in that thought and was involved in its execution. He is not a late arrival on the scene, showing his power for the first time at Pentecost following Christ's resurrection.

The birth of Jesus, the years of his ministry, the terrifying crucifixion and stunning resurrection comprise an incredible series of events in which each stage leads to another of even greater significance. This doesn't end with the resurrection. A new chapter dawns, one in which the daily physical sight of Jesus gives way to his permanent, though invisible, presence in the lives of his followers. Jesus promised the Holy Spirit who would empower them for the rest of their lives.

THE INDWELLING PRESENCE

The Apostle Paul wrote, 'You are on the spiritual level, if only God's Spirit dwells within you; and if a man does not possess the Spirit of Christ, he is no Christian' (Romans 8:9). That seems pretty definitive to me. In other words, if I say I am a Christian I'm not claiming to be perfect, but I am witnessing to the presence of God's Holy Spirit in my life. Without that I have no right to make the claim.

And how does the Spirit choose whom he indwells? The amazing truth is that he waits to be invited in. Those who sincerely ask for the Spirit's presence and power receive it. The experience of millions of Christians over the centuries proves it to be true.

IN ME!

Spirit of Jesus, Guest of the soul,
Transforming Spirit, making us whole,
Come to your servant, so people see
Something of Jesus,
Jesus in me!

Spirit of Jesus, Spirit Divine,
All I surrender, all that was mine,
Renew my nature, so there can be
Something of Jesus,
Jesus in me!

Spirit of Jesus, make this your hour.
Mine the obedience; yours is the pow'r.
I am your temple, now there shall be
Something of Jesus,
Jesus in me!

THE WARFARE

When the Teacher from Nazareth began his ministry he soon attracted opposition. Sometimes it took the form of bitter antagonism. Today's followers of Christ also attract opposition, to a greater or lesser degree. Martin Luther King Jr had enemies and died at the hand of one of them. Even the saintly Mother Teresa of Calcutta, who gave herself unstintingly in service to the very poor, was criticised cruelly at times. When the Salvation Army was re-established in one of the Eastern European countries following the fall of the Iron Curtain, the mayor of one of the major cities made life unbearable for those who took soup to the most poor.

Those who are mocked, or worse, suffer for their faith follow in the footsteps of Christ. They need our prayers. And those prayers should be for both our nearest and dearest and those who live on the other side of the world. And we should pray for ourselves, too. We all have to stand up and declare what we believe to an unsympathetic audience sometimes, if only to an audience of one. It can be costly.

At such times we should remember we are never alone. The Holy Spirit, God's Encourager, will help us. Jesus promised: 'When the Counsellor comes, whom I will send you from the Father, the Spirit of Truth who goes out from the Father, he will testify about me. And you also must testify' (John 15:26–27). This promise is both a comfort and a challenge.

TRANSFORMING POWER

An immediate change came over the disciples following their baptism by the Holy Spirit at Pentecost. Upper rooms with locked doors were no more. Now everything was very public, with praise freely offered to God for what they were achieving in his name. The changes were personalised in Peter. The disciple who had denied his association with Jesus became a courageous leader and confident speaker to crowds. Could any man be more transformed than Peter? The fact that some three thousand were added to their number on the day of Pentecost must have confirmed Peter's new resolve, both immediately and in the trying days and years that lay ahead.

Nobody was untouched as they dedicated themselves to teaching, to fellowship, to prayer, to the breaking of bread. In Colossians 3:12 we read, 'As God's chosen people, holy and dearly loved, clothe yourselves with compassion, kindness, humility, gentleness and patience.' What a beautiful picture that gives us of the kind of people God wants us to be, and longs to help us be! Not supermen and wonder-women, but people determinedly united in a quest to be—with the Holy Spirit's help—Christlike, holy.

I invite you to pray with me, both for ourselves and our beloved Army, this chorus from one of my songs:

Holy Spirit, promised presence fall on me.
Holy Spirit, make me all I long to be.
Holy Spirit, Holy spirit,
Give your pow'r to me, O Holy Spirit.

GENERAL JOHN GOWANS (Rtd) was known for his compelling platform ministry and his legacy of enduring lyrics from 10 full-length stage musicals co-authored with John Larsson. He has written three books of prayer poems and his autobiography. He with his wife Gisèle served in corps in the British Territory for 16 years, before being appointed national stewardship secretary. Following divisional leadership he became chief secretary in France, then followed leadership positions in the USA Western Territory and territorial leadership in France, Australia Eastern, and in 1997 the United Kingdom. In 1999 he was elected General. He holds an honorary doctorate from Yonsei University in Korea, and was given the Freedom of the City of London in 2000. Following retirement in 2002 he authored from 2007 to 2008 the Army's international devotional book, from which this chapter, with the author's permission, is excerpted (May 2007).

20

ECUMENISM

COMMISSIONER ELIZABETH A. MATEAR

My recent journey in ecumenical circles has been a high privilege. In April 2007 I was elected as moderator and public face of the Free Church Council, comprising 22 denominations and at the same time became co-president of Churches Together in England, the first Salvationist to hold the role. Involvement at this level allows for regular dialogue and conversations with colleague denominational heads—the Archbishop of Canterbury, from the Anglican Communion, the Archbishop of Westminster, Roman Catholic and the Orthodox Archbishop. As patron of more than a hundred groups with a Christian and interfaith focus, this affords me a breadth of ecumenical exposure. That is by way of my introduction to the current ecumenical scene and an indicator of the journey over the last one hundred years or so from the Salvation Army's beginnings. Salvation Army work and witness has not always been comfortable and smooth in its interaction with other members of the Body of Christ over the years.

Allow me a personal reflection from an interchurch celebration which took place in Westminster Abbey, London. As leader of the Free Churches I was required to lead the procession of clergy. Before moving off the verger turned and said, 'He would have been so proud today' as he pointed to the sculpted image of William Booth high in the cathedral wall. It seemed that the place of The Salvation Army at the centre of the nation's religious life and as part of the Body of Christ had become evident and relevant.

Ecumenism, the visible unity of the Church, is biblically right and therefore needs to be a goal to pursue. It concerns unity of the worldwide Church. The unity prayed for by the Lord Jesus in John 17:20–23 calls for a common life. Archbishop William Temple states, 'The way to a union of Christendom does not lie through committee rooms. It lies through personal union with the Lord, so deep and real as to be comparable with the Father.'

John 17, known to us as 'the high priestly prayer', is aspirational—'that they may be one'—firstly to bring glory to God and that they may be one so that others might come to faith, that the world might know that Jesus came from God and God loves the world, that they all may be one (v. 20, 23).

In 2000 years of Church history we have divided and evolved, from Acts 2 and beyond, to Orthodox, Roman, Eastern, Coptic, Anglican, Lutheran, Reformed, Dissenting Churches, Protestant, Charismatic and every nuance emanating from each one, including ourselves, The Salvation Army. It has been said that 'the divided church is an open wound in the body of Christ'. Rowan Williams, Archbishop of Canterbury, further comments, 'To say that the unity of the Church is sacramental reminds us that this is more than a unity of what we think or of what we do. It is a unity of divine invitation.'

In the present day we are more pluralistic in culture than ever. The gospel and the prayer of Jesus is about reconciliation, restoration, unity, witness and evangelism: 'My prayer is not for them alone. I pray also for those who will believe in me through their message… May they be brought to complete unity to let the world know that you sent me and have loved them even as I have loved you.' The divine intention is for the Church to be global in its scope and missional in its intention.

As a personal observation: Churches (denominations) tend to acquire their image or identity by geography (e.g. Eastern Orthodox, Roman, Church of England/India/Australia), by doctrine (e.g. Baptist or Pentecostal etc.) or by a person (Lutheran, Wesleyan). The differences appear to be those of doctrine, history or practice.

By name The Salvation Army has a clear and unbounded opportunity for global mission. We are The (only one)—Salvation (our mission)—Army (our strength and organisation).

Church organisation, doctrine and structure apart, we want to stand up for the dignity of every human being created in God's image. The Church exists to bring the world into the knowledge of Jesus and the love of God. The message of salvation is authentic when it contributes toward reconciling people, nations and culture. As we come together with our brothers and sisters in Christ we recognise and respect the ingredients of nationality, culture, denomination, theological belief and even program emphasis. In the presence of God's Holy Spirit of truth we need to be humble and open to be challenged and changed, otherwise discord will result. We must use our diversity as an asset. Division is a liability to a watching world. We would be wrong to ignore or minimise these, rather we give them the oxygen of debate. What divides us is not always theological. One of the most church-dividing issues has been race. That's partly a theological point, but it's also cultural and historical. Churches tend to be divided on moral and social issues, which often are discussed theologically, but which are rooted more in sociological and demographic factors. If we're not engaging these we are not doing the work.

Differences and distinctions need to be seen as either biblical or part of the evolving ecclesiastical tradition. Always paramount is the truth we have in common, the gospel. The recent history of ecumenism has offered numerous statements of intention and within fallible humanity there is a reiteration of the faith we profess and the mission we must pursue.

General Eva Burrows held office during Lausanne II—The International Congress on World Evangelisation. In 1989 the theme 'Calling the whole Church to take the whole gospel to the whole world' was endorsed by The Salvation Army as we projected our mission to 2000 and beyond. The covenant embraced then recognised the unfinished task of evangelisation, God's purpose to make himself known, the relevance of the Bible as God's Word, Jesus as the only Saviour of the world, the need to communicate the good news of salvation, Christian discipleship and the commitment of the Church to justice and reconciliation and challenging of injustice where it exists. As the Church, the community of God's people, comes together there is a renewed intention that we pray together, study together and work together. There is a difference between doing ecumenical things and doing things ecumenically. The ecumenical heart needs to be united in witness, in fellowship and work. We are hopefully long past any sense that we should do our own thing. God has given us everything we need and therefore we have resources to share, experiences to enrich and encouragement to give that will build us up. The diversity that is God's gift provides strength and blessing and calls us to intentionally work together in partnership to facilitate not only the spreading and expanding of the gospel but the deepening of truth in the lives of God's people. In this we share a common life in our richness and diversity.

Ecumenism must go beyond structures or organisation. The World Council of Churches has a helpful statement, 'Making a difference, together'. In this and in every generation we can please God if we continue to 'make every effort to keep the unity of the Spirit through the bond of peace' (Ephesians 4:3).

'Unity is not singing in unison and losing our distinctiveness; unity is singing in harmony, each person and tradition enriching the others.'

The Church should never be defined solely in terms of its activities as an institution, but always in terms of the character and purpose that it receives from God through grace. The ultimate goal is God's glory. Our ecumenical journey is an ongoing experience, as we participate and witness a living and ongoing interaction in every expression of church/community life, whether it be local or universal. It will impact our relationships and structures and certainly call for courage, commitment, wisdom and perseverance. It is hard work.

The key is to understand the meaning of Paul's words, which we gladly share when we say the grace: 'The grace of our Lord Jesus Christ, the love of God and the fellowship of the Holy Spirit be with us all evermore.'

TOGETHER IN A COMMON LIFE

O God, Holy and Eternal Trinity,
We pray for your Church in all the world.
Sanctify its life; renew its worship;
Empower its witness; heal its divisions;
Make visible its unity.
Lead us, with all our brothers and sisters,
Towards communion in faith, life and witness
So that, united in one body by the one Spirit,
We may together witness to the perfect unity of your love.

(From the constitutional guidelines for congregations in covenanted
partnership, by Churches Together in England)

COMMISSIONER ELIZABETH A. MATEAR, after commissioning in 1977, was responsible for the Army's alcoholic assessment unit in London. After marriage to John, their joint service was spent in the United Kingdom as corps officers, divisional youth secretaries and territorial church growth consultants. From 2001 until 2006, they served as territorial leaders for the Caribbean Territory, and in 2007 as territorial leaders of the United Kingdom Territory. In 2007 Commissioner Matear was elected moderator of the Free Churches in England and Wales. In addition she is co-president of Churches Together in England and patron to numerous groups and charities, with interfaith dialogue and engagement with government. God's equipping for ministry with spiritual gifts includes teaching, pastoring, evangelism, admin-istration and leadership.

21

APOSTOLIC OPTIMISM

LIEUT-COLONEL RICHARD MUNN

'Optimism is the faith that leads to achievement.
Nothing can be done without hope and confidence.'
—Helen Keller

It was intended as an insult. But he wore it with pride—'an enthusiast'. And the evangelical world has never been the same since. Thank you, John Wesley.[1]

It is axiomatic that nothing of worth is ever truly accomplished in this world without conviction and passion. Entrepreneurs, athletes and artists know this intuitively. Religious leaders, it seems, tend to be more temperate. So, let us ponder for a moment this matter of 'apostolic optimism'. Is there a biblical precedent? Could it be that Christians in general, and Salvationists in particular, are called to exude the power of Christ-centric optimism in the dark and difficult places of our beautiful world?

It is heartening to note that 'enthusiast' literally means 'in God'—*en theos*. Presumably during the mystery of language formation the ancient lovers of God exhibited some notable fervour.

Similarly with 'optimism'. While not strictly a biblical word, its etymology fits well the ethos of Scripture—from the French optimisme, 'the greatest good'; Latin, optimus—'the best'.[2]

Thus, *Apostolic Optimism* is seeing the best, the greatest good, and exuding this perspective to such a degree that new territories and new culture-breaching movements are enacted for the cause of the gospel. It is power of remarkable degree, one that counters opposition, and rallies significant numbers of people to do the same. Much more than mere 'positive thinking', apostolic optimism wins people groups and establishes

---

[1] Henry Rack, *Reasonable Enthusiast: John Wesley and the Rise of Methodism*, Epworth Press, 2002

[2] Ernest Weekley, *An Etymological Dictionary of Modern English,* Dover Publications, 1967

territory for the Kingdom of God—in sometimes the most barren and inhospitable terrain. 'No pessimist ever discovered the secrets of the stars, or sailed to an uncharted land, or opened a new heaven to the human spirit,' wrote Helen Keller.

BIBLICAL OPTIMISTS

Nowhere is this more vividly depicted than the Old Testament account of Moses sending the 12 spies to reconnoitre newly-promised Canaan— 'a good and spacious land flowing with milk and honey'. Palpable fear saturates the final report.

In the midst of this unbelief two men exude confidence—Caleb and Joshua: 'If the Lord is pleased with us, he will lead us into that land…and will give it to us… Do not be afraid of the people of the land, because we will swallow them up. Their protection is gone, but the Lord is with us. Do not be afraid of them' (Numbers 14:7–9). Note the optimism. In fact, the Lord himself pronounces that Caleb and his descendants will inherit the land, because 'my servant Caleb has a different spirit and follows me wholeheartedly' (Numbers 14:24). We could say that Caleb has 'apostolic optimism'. He is an enthusiast.

Centuries later this same quality percolates in Paul and Silas while imprisoned in Philippi. It is no mere joie de vivre that empowers these early incarcerated and shackled apostles to pray and sing hymns to God at midnight—following a 'severe flogging' no less (Acts 16:23,25). This is powerful optimism. The outcome is a miracle, the salvation of the jailer and his family, prison release and the understandable 'encouragement' of the local congregation. Anointed effervescence secures another beachhead for the gospel.

THE CORPORATE MODEL

Like so many other rich biblical principles, the cut and thrust of the corporate world shrewdly embraces the power of optimism for entrepreneurial success. This is frequently asserted as a factor in both personal growth and commercial development. The very essence of free enterprise is to capitalise possibilities. The general consensus is that optimism results in higher achievement.

Norman Vincent Peale inaugurated an entire philosophy and movement with his 1950s bestseller *The Power of Positive Thinking*. Written in the aftermath of global war, his capacity to point upwards and outwards lifted thousands of people around the world.

Stephen Covey lists 'thinking win-win' as one of his Seven Habits of Highly Effective People. He says it requires a combination of empathy and confidence, being considerate and exhibiting bravery. He also applies the principle to effective organisations. That combination seems uncannily applicable to the mission of The Salvation Army—compassion and courage.[3]

Commissioner Robert Watson quotes best-known management theorist Peter Drucker who describes The Salvation Army in the Commissioner's book titled *The Most Effective Organization in the United States* as just that. The final chapter is simply entitled 'Make Joy Count.' Drucker sees this dynamism as a corporate distinction, one of the irrepressible reasons for the continuing success of The Salvation Army around the world.[4]

THE SALVATION ARMY

The Archbishop of Canterbury, Michael Ramsey, seemed to sense this during the pivotal 1965 Centenary Congress in London. In the presence of HRH Queen Elizabeth II, General Frederick Coutts, territorial leaders and thousands of Salvationists gathered in the Royal Albert Hall, he made a quite remarkable statement.

> It's wonderful to think of the variety of qualities and gifts that must be brought together in such a gathering from every part of the world, but there's one gift that I believe every Salvationist has in a wonderful measure and that is the gift of joy. I've seen many odd things in my time. I don't think I've ever seen a gloomy member of The Salvation Army. The gift of joy is very wonderfully yours and may that gift go on being yours.[5]

In some sense this buoyancy should come as no surprise. From the very

---

[3] Stephen R. Covey, *The Seven Habits of Highly Effective People*, Simon & Schuster Ltd; 15th Anniversary Edition, 2004

[4] Robert Watson, *The Most Effective Organisation in the US: Leadership Secrets of the Salvation Army*, Carown Business, New York, 2001

[5] *Into The Second Century,* Salvationist Publishing, London, 1965

outset William and Catherine Booth exhibited a commanding capacity to see beyond the deprivations of immediate circumstances, and to contagiously rally people to join them.

In one remarkable address to the International Staff Council, 1904, General William Booth described his vision for the future of The Salvation Army. It centred on '*a new body of officers*':

> As I looked at this new people, they appeared to manifest extraordinary signs of earnestness, self-denial, and singleness of purpose; indeed, they had every appearance of being a reckless, daredevil set... They seemed to welcome privations, and to revel in hardships, counting it all joy when they fell into diverse persecutions, and facing opposition and difficulties with meekness, patience, and love... Do you ask me about their support? Oh! I answer, so far as I could find out in my dream, they never lacked any really necessary thing, having all the time what was above all and beyond all in worth and desirability—the abundant smile of God, and a great harvest of precious souls.[6]

Talk about apostolic optimism!

One of the distinctive features of an apostle is the capacity to sally the gospel across cultural boundary lines. Such endeavours are not for the faint of heart, and should not be embarked upon lightly. Even the most godly, confident optimism will be severely tested. Without the clear direction of God, not a few sorties into uncharted territory have floundered painfully. Even with divine directional clarity, it seems, timing is everything. Such a moment occurred in recent Salvation Army history.

At the end of the 1980s the Soviet Union suddenly disintegrated. In spontaneous reaction the people of Eastern Europe and Russia exhibited genuine receptivity to the gospel. Cultures that had lived for decades under official atheism were now much more open and accessible. The General of The Salvation Army, Eva Burrows, sensed the potential of the moment. 'I believe there is great opportunity for the gospel in Eastern Europe today,' she said. 'After the cynical disillusionment with Communist philosophy,

---

[6] William Booth, *International Staff Council Addresses*, 1904

there is a spiritual vacuum and people have their hearts open to the Gospel.'[7]

The rest is history. Apostolic optimism coursed through a new generation of pioneer leaders—Salvationists around the world even—and ultimately created new boundary lines for The Salvation Army, lines that would have seemed unthinkable just a decade before. Burrows' biographer Henry Gariepy concludes: 'The advance and reopening of the Army in these communist bloc countries was a high solstice of General Burrows' term. With vision and vigour she advanced the Army into new frontiers in Liberia, El Salvador, Czechoslovakia, Hungary, Latvia and Russia.'[8]

Apostolic optimism will exude only from a few individuals, and be characteristic in a few movements. Could it be that this special empowerment is to be a defining hallmark of The Salvation Army; that in the dark, inhospitable and neglected places of our world, this Army of joyful optimism is especially assigned?

'Joy! Joy! Joy! There is joy in The Salvation Army!' May it ever be so!

---

[7] Henry Gariepy, *General of God's Army*, Victor Books, 1993

[8] *op cit*

LIEUT-COLONEL RICHARD MUNN is a fourth-generation Salvationist. Born in London, he spent the first 10 years of his life in the Congo where his parents were missionary teachers. During his student years, he participated in an exchange program through which he worked at a USA Army summer camp where he met his future wife, Janet. He has earned a bachelor degree in education, masters in divinity, and a doctor of ministry degree. The Munns served in corps, youth ministry, divisional leadership and then as territorial program secretary in the USA East. In 2008 he assumed responsibility as principal for the newly named International College for Officers and Centre for Spiritual Life Development in London. He also serves as secretary for international ecumenical relations, is a member of the international doctrine council, and has been a contributor to Army periodicals.

SECTION 3

TO SERVE
SUFFERING HUMANITY

22

HUMAN TRAFFICKING

COMMISSIONER HELEN CLIFTON

On 31 October 2004, a 16-year-old Lithuanian girl made the greatest mistake of her life when she agreed to go to London with some boys for a 'Hallowe'en treat'. They turned out to be part of a trafficking gang who then intimidated her and forced her into prostitution. Eventually located and rescued after many months, she was badly damaged and her life would never be the same. The perpetrators were prosecuted and in December 2005, they received prison sentences of 18 and 14 years (*BBC News Online*).

Multiply this two million times a year and you have a concept of how many people are trapped, tricked and taken far from their familiar surroundings on a worldwide basis.

Sex trade trafficking is a particular focus for The Salvation Army's concern and has been from the earliest days. Bramwell and Florence Booth, part of the 'second generation' of Salvation Army leaders, became aware of child sex exploitation when they themselves were young parents. The 24-year-old Florence held her second baby in her arms when she sat in court in 1885 watching her husband wrongly accused for his part in exposing the sex crimes, through the Eliza Armstrong case, along with W.T. Stead (editor of the *Pall Mall Gazette*), Rebecca Jarrett (a former prostitute) and Madame Mourez (a midwife of doubtful repute). The story is told in *For Such a Time* by Lieut-Colonel Jenty Fairbank, with close reference to original journal sources, which are often very moving.

Their efforts raised the age of consent in the UK to 16 years of age (Criminal Law Amendment Act, 1885). However, even this was undermined by the United Kingdom Sexual Offences Act, 2003, which declared *belief* that a child aged 13–16 was 'older than 16' to be a possible valid defence against a child rape charge. The battles are not over and there is an ongoing need for vigilance. Young girls and boys are still enticed and coerced into prostitution all over the world.

Modern 'Florence Booths' include Lisa L. Thompson of USA National Headquarters, who has spearheaded powerful coalitions and campaigns, and Dianna Bussey, who works on diversion programs with male sex offenders in Winnipeg, Canada. Like Lisa, she has participated in formal and influential submissions to government, resulting in changes to the law and increased resources for work with trafficked individuals. Lisa's team includes Katie Luse, who travels and teaches, and because of her youth can relate to the young women of the world. Women like Mrs Swarna de Silva in Sri Lanka, Mrs Chris Frazer in New Zealand, Majors Wendy Leavey and Teresa Baah in Ghana, Dr Mariana Rojas in Argentina, Gun-Viv Glad-Jungner in Finland, Major (Dr) SallyAnn Hood in Mexico and many more—some of whose work with victims is too confidential to mention—stand together in healthy and determined opposition to commercial sex exploitation. They constitute a Salvation Army network that stretches right around the world, loosely linked but capable of cooperation when needed.

Lieut-Colonel Dawn Sewell, who headed the anti-trafficking desk in London and now works intensively with the UK Territory in combating trafficking, brings her nursing and emergency response aptitudes to a field which is indeed urgent, unpredictable and requires rapid response. Commissioner Christina Kjellgren brought together a network of European Salvationists in a networking conference at The Salvation Army's international headquarters. Commissioner Christine MacMillan (International Social Justice Commission) is a powerful advocate for justice on a global basis and, as a woman of God and an experienced social worker, she finds the fight against trafficking is high on her agenda.

PREVENTION, PROTECTION, PROSECUTION AND PRAYER

The work is done on various levels. Prevention, protection, prosecution and prayer are all important weapons in our armory against evil.

Prevention includes awareness-raising and educational programs. It also involves research and advocacy for legal frameworks that will ease the work of the police and immigration services in intervention. Tackling the demand for commercial sex is difficult but essential, as the men who purchase sex on a regular basis (many of them family men) learn the real implications of their demand for gratification.

Protection dovetails with prevention and extends to the safe care of those survivors of trafficking who have actually been rescued. Resources are needed to provide high-level residential care, with language support, counselling and legal advice on hand. The USA, United Kingdom, Australia, Sri Lanka and Malawi territories/commands are already making their contribution, and other places are also well ahead with plans. As awareness is raised, so funding is given, from the generous hearts of Salvationists, donor friends and government grants to support this expensive work. Who can put a price on a woman's life? Who would really want to 'get rid of the problem' by deporting her to her country of origin, where she is only vulnerable to retrafficking?

Prosecution is a deterrent to trafficking gangs. What can The Salvation Army do here? The answers include: advocate for tough sentences for perpetrators; keep sex trade trafficking high on the agenda of police and government agencies; and protect and rehabilitate traumatised victims so they have a chance of giving evidence. The latter takes time and patience, plus legal provision for visas—for women damaged within our countries and by 'our' men. The Salvation Army's seriousness in advocacy and hands-on help to victims give us a useful and credible voice.

Finally, all the above strategies need prayer support because, as the Bible reminds us, 'the weapons of our warfare are not carnal' (2 Corinthians 10:4) and we are engaged in fighting 'spiritual wickedness in high places' (Ephesians 6:12).

It is hoped that with the creation of the International Social Justice Commission in New York (part of international headquarters but located just a few blocks from the United Nations) those working in related fields in many countries will feel even more supported and empowered. Commissioner Christine MacMillan directs the ISJC, with Lieut-Colonel Geanette Seymour and Major Victoria Edmonds at the heart of her team.

As one who has role-modelled Christian womanhood throughout her life, General Eva Burrows would definitely applaud this work. She has served in Sri Lanka and Zimbabwe, knowing how vulnerable young women and children are in their beauty and poverty. As General, she drove forward The Salvation Army's advances into Russia and the former Soviet Union—understanding how its joyful, passionate, purposeful, sacrificial ministry would be needed in lands now free but battling poverty and wide open to the expansion of the sex and gambling industries. She has also served as head of women's social services in the United Kingdom, an appointment which brought her face to face with the outcasts and rejects of society—the victims of addictions and the damaged, discarded, once-beautiful survivors of prostitution.

Living in retirement in Melbourne, she attends a downtown corps with a ministry to the marginalised. She is still a notable speaker and a voice for the voiceless—those whose plight society tends to confine to the 'too hard' box, but for whom The Salvation Army still intercedes, with tears, in the presence of Jesus Christ.

COMMISSIONER HELEN CLIFTON upon election of her husband, Shaw Clifton, as General in 2006, became world president of women's ministries. She earned a BA in English language and literature and a postgraduate certificate of education. She and her husband served as corps officers in the United Kingdom, and in Zimbabwe at Mazowe Secondary School and as corps officers. They served as leaders for Pakistan, New Zealand, Fiji and Tonga as well as leaders of the UK Territory with the Republic of Ireland, and earlier as divisional leaders in the USA. She has been chair of the Pakistan Territory's human resources development board, and was also director of the Army's nationwide mother and child health education (MACHE) project in Pakistan. She was a facilitator/contributor to the Army's international summit on poverty. In the UK she had headed a territorial task force to respond to human trafficking, with innovative programs devised and piloted to support women leaving the sex trade.

23

SALVATIONISM IN ACTION

COMMISSIONER HOPE MUNGATE

If all resources were at my disposal I still could not do justice to this exciting festschrift, felicitating Salvation war veteran General Eva Burrows. However, given limited resources, I cannot fail to put down on paper something for this publication.

The Oxford Dictionary defines Salvationism as a 'militancy model for charity and revival of Christianity among the destitute by Salvationists'. The Salvation Army has succeeded in meeting this goal worldwide, skewed more towards charity that has earned the trust of peoples around the world.

Since its inception The Salvation Army has concerned itself with propagating the gospel that is summed up in the phrase 'Heart to God and hand to man'. The first part of this phrase has been the driving force for the latter. All social endeavours are motivated by the Army's spiritual purpose. The Army's social centres around the world resonate with powerful stories of transformed lives through the saving grace of Christ that have been celebrated. These miracles come from the spectrum of Army's schools, hospitals, clinics, homes for elderly, children's homes, mother and toddler programs, orphanages, abused girls homes, delinquency reformatory homes, rehabilitation of former prostitutes, feeding schemes, work with refugees, prisoners rehabilitation work, etc.

In Africa Salvationism has developed using schools, hospitals and clinics as an entry point to the saving of souls. The pioneers and their successors saw the need of educating their converts through the medium of schools, while at the same time realising that medical centres had to be set up to reach those who had physical needs. Replicating such important social programs necessitated the rise of training schools for nurses and teachers. These training-of-trainers' centres became very important as they churned out more and more professionals to serve in both urban and remote areas. Salvationism touched the lives of millions of young people who passed through our schools and college, and many who received training and treatment at Army hospitals and clinics. Salvationism has developed over the years in such a way that it has permeated and positively influenced many people within the regions of Africa.

Undaunted by their monumental task, with great determination and spirit of sacrifice, 'overseas missionaries' and their national counterparts have bravely fought and conquered the dark world of their time. Denying themselves of desire for comfort and fame they served the Lord wholeheartedly knowing that their reward will be in heaven. They fed themselves on food of the local people and slept in discomfort for the sake of spreading God's love. Our international leaders have recognised them as people of integrity and often with capacity to serve in a position to touch the whole Army world from International Headquarters and in senior appointments elsewhere.

The 17 years of General Eva Burrows' early service in Zimbabwe can be clearly reviewed in retrospect as time well invested in effectively improving Salvationism in that country. Classroom instruction displayed a marked difference between her commitment to teaching students and that of those employed for remuneration. This is confirmed today as her former students talk about the love they saw in General Burrows both in the formal classroom and outdoor settings. The majority of students who studied under her influence at Howard and Usher Institutes testify with great joy that what they are today is as the direct result of her efforts to help them achieve a better quality of life. Some of her students became teachers, nurses, medical doctors, policemen and national army personnel, while others branched out into industry and diplomatic service. Not only did she influence her students toward success in society, but also to become colleagues in the teaching profession and emulate her lifestyle in becoming prominent Salvationists. Some have already gone to glory but many are still serving the Lord faithfully in their advanced years as good Salvationists.

In all her officership Eva Burrows demonstrated her desire to develop Salvationism. This intention is the spirit of the Army and the desire of every Salvationist that we should be an Army of high quality with that quality reflected in soldiership among the people. William Booth's statement 'Some of my best men are women' rightly applies to the accomplishments of General Burrows enabled by the Holy Spirit. Committed Salvationists arc achicving thc goals for which thc Army was raiscd by God.

The world has never been so ready to be served by the word of God, with its natural and man-made disasters devastating human lives and God's creation. The slogan given by Winston Churchill, 'Where there is need there is The Salvation Army' has found it turning disaster into God's fortune. The rapid response to floods in the USA, Bangladesh, Sri Lanka, India, Mozambique and many other places is a demonstration of its Salvationism to the world. Its services to the people of war-torn Iraq, Sudan and Afghanistan show that love knows no fear.

In Kivu, in the eastern part of the Democratic Republic of Congo where civil war has played havoc with innocent lives, a small group of Salvationists from nearby corps, without fear, has counselled the women and young girls who have been raped and abused by rebels. This quality of Salvationism has never been so necessary as it is today. The world is 'groaning like a woman in childbirth' because of suffering of the whole creation. The integrity of creation is ignored and its sanctity violated by the evils and sin of man. They give no regard for orphans, widows, aliens and suffering humanity. In fact, these vulnerable groups of people are taken as cheap prey for sharks and abusers of mankind.

There has been a shift in the world, drifting from listening to the Church's voice to that of the politician. Our world is in deep trouble and in need of Christ the Saviour, the Liberator and righteous King. The Salvation Army has a powerful message from God to the world through its complete service to mankind—soul-saving and charity. Our governments, members of parliament, mayors of cities, and all in positions of leadership need to be reminded of God's requirements for their leadership on behalf of their citizens.

Our experience in Nigeria during the religious clashes between Christians and Muslims taught us a major lesson. We never knew that the Muslims were watching the way the Salvationists behave themselves in the community of Jos in Plateau State. In 2005 when a serious clash erupted between Christians and Muslims, many church buildings and mosques were destroyed by angry Christians and Muslims retaliating against those of different faith. Our divisional commander then was staying in Jos using Jos Corps premises. It was the Muslim imam who rescued the family of our divisional commander and protected the building of The Salvation Army against being destroyed by militant Muslims. When an enquiry was made to find out why the imam protected the Army property and its divisional leader, Muslims replied that The Salvation Army is not an enemy of anybody, therefore their people and property should not be touched, but protected.

I want to believe that this is the same reason that The Salvation Army has been accepted to serve in Iraq, Kuwait and Sudan. Salvationism creates an open door for greater and special service. It is possible that in the near future The Salvation Army will march into many of those countries where it is not yet known and established. It has the capacity to achieve more, given human and financial resources.

It is unarguably true that 'an army rises and falls by its leadership'. Therefore, for Salvationism to make the desired impact, personnel to effect this agenda should be well-versed in its theology. Training of personnel has no substitute. Times are changing, therefore our training colleges' syllabuses need to match the challenges of the moment to keep our personnel relevant, effective and efficient. Internationalism of The Salvation Army can play a special role through the sharing of personnel worldwide. The Western world has been giving of its human and financial resources since the beginning; now is time for the developing world to share its spiritual resources. Already there are those from the developing world who have responded to the challenge to serve in West where their unique gifts will develop the spirit of Salvationism along new frontiers of service for God.

Developing Salvationism calls for total commitment on the part of all Salvationists, adherents and friends, despite the insecurity brought about by world terrorism. Salvationism has been a hallmark of the Army since its origin, and now more than ever it needs to be kept pure and expanded in our world of deep need. Let us rise to the challenge.

COMMISSIONER HOPE MUNGATE, a Zimbabwean, and her husband Stuart served as territorial leaders for Nigeria, and are currently leaders in Congo and Angola Territory (due to retire in December 2009). She is the president of women's organisations and editor and literary secretary. They formerly served in the Democratic Republic of Congo. She had been chaplain at the Army's Howard Hospital and supervised the weaving and dressmaking school. Appointments in the Army's social work, training college, education, corps and youth work were also filled with distinction. She attended the International College for Officers, has written three books in the Shona vernacular and two in English, studied journalism and communication, and serves on ecumenical church councils.

24

SOCIAL JUSTICE

CAPTAIN DANIELLE STRICKLAND

'Is this not the kind of fasting I have chosen: to loose the chains of injustice and untie the cords of the yoke, to set the oppressed free and break every yoke? Is it not to share your food with the hungry and to provide the poor wanderer with shelter—when you see the naked, to clothe him, and not to turn away from your own flesh and blood?'

These words in Isaiah 58:6 made William Booth's heart beat faster. The prophetic inclination towards justice was enough to shape his life and fuel his ministry into world-shaping activities. This exegetical texture of biblical justice within our movement is a hidden catalyst towards holy revolution. Yet, how do we break it down into achievable parts that make sense? Can we get from the 'what' to the 'how' of social justice and impact the world?

Gunilla Ekberg is a social reformer from Sweden who in recent history managed to turn the reality of oppression through prostitution around by legislating new approaches to deal with root issues surrounding violence against women. And in doing this, she dealt a nearly fatal blow to human traffickers in Sweden. At one point in the process the Swedish government declared on its website, 'We want the world to know that in Sweden women and children are not for sale.'

I asked her how she did it. She gave me two essential ingredients to world-changing behaviour, and these get us straight to the heart of social justice.

ESSENTIAL ONE: IMAGINE A BETTER WORLD

Gunilla and her friends would gather together and imagine a world where women didn't have to sell their bodies for sex in order to eat. They simply started the reform process by using their imaginations to envision a country that actually took care of the most oppressed people within it.

Remarkably, it seems every social reformer I've read about did the same thing. William Booth simply wrote his imaginings down in his manifesto, *In Darkest England and The Way Out*—and its release caused quite a stir. Imagine England without poverty.

He's not alone. William Wilberforce imagined a world without slavery (he was with a small company of fellow visionaries at the start). Martin Luther King Jr could envisage (and often did—out loud) a world without racial prejudice. Elizabeth Fry could visualise a prison system that was about reform.

The Salvation Army has the potential to 're-imagine' the world. We were born into this. We don't have to join the naysayers of moral policing, and we certainly don't belong in the 'rapture rescue' party, spending our time and energy protecting ourselves from darkness while the world goes to hell. No, that is not for us! Paul suggests that the only way to get out of conformity to the world's mould (whose squeezing grip becomes ever more inevitable) is to renew our minds in the Kingdom: 'Do not conform any longer to the pattern of this world but be transformed by the renewing of your mind' (Romans 12:1). True social justice begins here.

Have we succumbed to 'managing darkness' instead of the greater task of envisioning the world without any darkness at all? Our mission is as prophetic as it is practical, and we will not achieve the former if we lose sight of our true calling. We are not moral police; we are not about religious conservatism; we are not in a popularity contest; nor is fundraising the ultimate goal. We are about the making of a better world. We are convinced that the Kingdom of God looks like hope, peace, love and joy invading the darkest places. We storm the forts and bring them down. We are the dreamers who can't live with pathetic, lukewarm compromises of washed-out grey religion in place of the presence of the true King. Or are we?

Jeffrey Sachs wrote the book *The End of Poverty* and helped develop the Millennium Development Goals for the UN (popularised in the global 'Make Poverty History' campaign). He's a dreamer. Is The Salvation Army able to imagine a world without people dying of hunger? Can we envisage the end of poverty through creative and flexible economic systems with the likes of Mohammad Yunis, declaring as he stood to receive his Nobel Peace Prize (2007) his belief that his grandchildren would have to visit a museum to see extreme poverty? He dreams as a Muslim of a better world, perhaps a living re-enactment of the Samaritan story made alive to us by its hopeful rebuke as we hold the secrets of the Kingdom of Christ and keep them to ourselves. Can we allow ourselves the prophetic liberty of imagining the end of human trafficking or the global equality of women? Can we see in our mind's eye the dismantling of industry standards that exploit children around the globe?

To engage in the discipline of non-conformity with the world, stalwartly refusing to agree with the enemy and to transform our thinking, yes even our dreaming to 'boundless salvation—the whole world redeeming' is the hope of social justice.

ESSENTIAL TWO: UNDERSTAND OPPRESSION

John Wesley suggested 'there is no holiness apart from social holiness' and William Booth said that Salvationism was simply this, 'the overcoming and banishing from the Earth of wickedness'. Biblical social justice is fulfilling Jesus' prayers by taking hold of heaven and bringing it to Earth. Jesus came to bring the Kingdom here and now and we are those who believe his presence is best expressed to the world with our sleeves rolled up and dirt under our nails.

We are hard workers. But hard work is not the answer in itself. There have been many occasions where a direct result of injustice is a poor understanding of oppression. Exploitation, oppression and injustice are often a complex layering of facts and systems. In order to get at the cause it takes time, energy and resources to dig to the foundation and hit it strategically, dismantling the whole thing. A popularised illustration explaining justice is the occasion when someone becomes so tired of pulling dead bodies out of the river they head upstream to see where they are falling in.

For The Salvation Army this is key to our warfare. How many of our services are similar to what we've done for decades? Locked in a traditional form of ministry to 'the poor' we can unknowingly participate in the very oppression we seek to destroy. The result of busy work without justice is a glimpse of oppression but not a proper understanding of it. Ekberg prophetically warns us in her essentials that if we do not figure out oppression we will not be able to create solutions to confront and dismantle it.

Again her advice is mirrored by other social reformers: Martin Luther King Jr struggled to relate to the young blacks of the North, confined to ghettos and moving towards violence and black power as an answer to their own feelings of oppression and injustice. Although he met with them to talk, he could not relate to their strong reactions against hope and love as a force to change the situation. In an attempt to understand, he moved into a Chicago slum. Mohammad Yunis spent over a year with the poorest of the poor in Bangladesh documenting their lives to understand their economic oppression. His conclusions are crumbling the foundations of injustice among impoverished women the world over. It wasn't until Gandhi began to shed the imperialism of the West and adopt a lifestyle of close proximity to India's poor that he gained the insight to challenge the colonial oppression of his people. God sent Jesus to live among us. Not only to challenge the oppression of sin, but to understand it completely and destroy it from the inside out.

If we are serious dreamers of a better world we need to spend time understanding oppression and planning for its defeat. A true grasp cannot be gleaned from a professional distance or a comfortable desk. An accurate picture is created from an incarnated presence; a knowing that is felt, experienced and absorbed completely. Even the small steps of deep insights are painful and costly. The early slum sisters of The Salvation Army valued their job to dismantle darkness from the inside out. William Booth understood oppression because he ventured to the wrong part of town and chose to see it. Bramwell Booth did something about child prostitution in London because his wife wept at the plight of the women caught in its clutches every night as they went to bed. We have impacted nations, countries and industry not because of friends in high places but because of friends in low places. We've understood oppression.

Will we rise to the new global challenge? There are giants who mock us at every turn; human traffickers exploiting women and children, addiction raging in city streets, abuse and human rights violations, extreme poverty robbing people of life itself. What will we do?

The essentials of social justice remind us and employ us. Will we lose ourselves, our small daytime dreams for God's Kingdom come? Will we draw close to that which repulses us in order to understand? Will we study the Kingdom and the world alike so one might impact the other? Will we prepare and strategise for justice to reign and roll? Will we be flexible enough to answer oppression with the necessary strategic blows, even if it doesn't look like much and costs us everything?

I imagine we will. Do you?

CAPTAIN DANIELLE STRICKLAND is currently the social justice director of the Australia Southern Territory, establishing teams of social justice representatives in each division and launching territorial campaigns and prayer initiatives and networks. She has co-authored books on social justice, leadership and soldier training. Isaiah 58 makes Danielle's heart beat faster. She helped found in Vancouver an inner city incarnational corps and The War College—a mission training school. She has earned her MA in leadership from Trinity Western University. She has enjoyed an international platform for speaking and teaching, in 15 countries. Married to Major Stephen Court, and the mother of two boys, she says, 'I love Jesus, and want to be more like him.'

25

A D D R E S S I N G   T H E   I S S U E S

G E N E R A L   J O H N   L A R S S O N   (R T D)

W A R   O N   A   T H O U S A N D   F R O N T S

No military general would relish the prospect of his army fighting on a thousand fronts. Yet The Salvation Army does just that, and very effectively. It is part of what makes the Army unique.

It all began when William Booth, returning late from an engagement outside London, saw the hundreds of men who slept huddled against the parapets on the bridges over the river Thames. The next morning he issued his orders to his chief of the staff, Bramwell Booth. 'Go and do something,' he said. And Bramwell did. Warehouses were obtained, beds were bought, and The Salvation Army's work with shelters and hostels for the homeless was born.

William Booth did not coin the slogan 'Where there's a need, there is The Salvation Army'. Sir Winston Churchill is given the credit for that. But the saying sums up to perfection William Booth's philosophy and the marching orders that he as commander-in-chief gave to his soldiers: 'Where there's a need, go and do something!'

By the mid-1880s William Booth had become utterly convinced that salvation had to be more than spiritual salvation; it had to be salvation of the whole person. 'I saw,' he wrote, 'that when the Bible said, "he that believeth shall be saved," it meant not only saved from the miseries of the future world, but from the miseries of this world as well.' The Army's mission was not only soul salvation but whole salvation.

Roger Green has well described this dual emphasis as a war on two fronts. But the battle to alleviate human suffering soon proved so diverse that it is no exaggeration to say that The Salvation Army today is at war on a thousand fronts.

When in Britain the early-day Salvation soldiers went to war with William Booth's orders ringing in their ears, every need they sought to alleviate opened up a new front. The Army established food kitchens for the hungry, sent slum officers into the inner cities to live among the deprived, housed the homeless, provided work and vocational training for the unemployed, established labour bureaus, took on the drink trade and combatted the scourge of alcoholism. It set up homes for orphaned children, opened eventide homes for the elderly, built maternity units for unmarried mothers, and pioneered services for the deaf and for the blind. It challenged industries that were exploiting their employees, helped prostitutes escape their way of life, and fought the white slave trade. It traced missing relatives, provided free legal advice, gave matrimonial counselling, and helped thousands to migrate and settle in new countries. It opened a bank for the poor and set up an insurance company for them. No need seemed too great or too small for the Army to tackle. Already it was war on a hundred fronts.

As the Army spread to other countries, the pioneers showed the same audacity. Many of the programs from the Army's country of birth were replicated around the world, but astonishing initiatives were also launched to meet the different needs of different countries.

In Australia, work among released prisoners was commenced. In India, the Army pioneered ministry to the untouchables. In Japan, Salvationists marched into the heart of Tokyo to attack prostitution. In Sweden and New Zealand, the Army purchased islands for the rehabilitation of alcoholics. In the USA, vast salvage programs provided relief, work, training and a return to society for thousands. In France, the Army shamed the nation into closing its penal colony on Devil's Island. In India and Africa, hospitals and clinics were opened. When war broke out the Army provided support for the troops, the Army's American doughnut girls becoming famous in World War I. Every country had its story to tell.

Today the satellites that spin around the globe look down on a Salvation Army that more than ever is following General William Booth's command to meet need with action. Salvation Army schools—with half a million pupils attending daily—Army clinics, HIV/AIDS health teams, ministry to refugees and migrants, feeding programs for the hungry, emergency and disaster relief, and support schemes for students, the lonely and the outcasts of society, are all part of that action. Through its projects system the Army digs wells, builds schools, opens new roads, gives training in agriculture and computing, and handles thousands of micro-credit programs. With its corps-based community care ministries the Army reaches out to over 16,000 communities in 118 countries around the world to care for the poor, feed the hungry, clothe the naked, love the unlovable, and befriend those who have no friends.

It truly is war on a thousand fronts.

'Where there's a need, there is The Salvation Army' is a gracious compliment, but a mind-boggling mission statement. Can any organisation be expected to meet *any* kind of need *any*where? Can a General of The Salvation Army successfully give overall strategic direction to a war that is being fought on so many and such diverse fronts?

Fortunately for all of William Booth's successors, his standing orders remain in place. Not for the Army the luxury of being a 'one issue' social service agency. The General therefore relies on the vision and good judgment of all territorial, divisional and corps/centre leaders around the world, together with the Salvationists they represent, to implement those standing orders according to the needs of each community and the available resources of finance and personnel. Choices have to be made, for even The Salvation Army—despite the compliments paid—cannot attempt to meet *every* need without exception in *every* place.

Getting the logistics into place for the war on a thousand fronts remains a never-ending task, and at the logistical apex stands the General. Some programs demand large capital investments in buildings and equipment. All programs demand ongoing financial resources—some on a vast scale. There are programs that can function only with specialist professionals with the necessary expertise—doctors, engineers, counsellors—while others can successfully work with trained volunteers. Securing the necessary continual flow of funding from internal and external sources, and the services of professionals and volunteers, is a demanding and complex undertaking. This in itself sets certain limitations on the needs that the Army can realistically tackle.

But the General is primarily called to be the prophet who scans the horizons, listens to those who are engaged on the front lines, and then, having discerned the new needs and the issues of the day, leads the Army into action.

Each General has done that, and General Eva Burrows outstandingly so. For most of her term she was not only the international leader but also the ultimate leader of the Army in Britain. With this dual responsibility, General Burrows, in her own direct and fearless fashion, focused the Army on the issues of racial segregation and abortion, the needs of women, the family, the unemployed, the homeless and those suffering from HIV/AIDS. And through the United Nation she addressed the issue of nuclear disarmament.

The future of this world of globalisation, mass migration and instant communication will bring its own challenges. Some of the old needs remain, but new ones will arise. Therefore the Army will ever be called to recognise and meet the changing needs of each community where it is at work. On the world scene, the Army's International Social Justice Commission, established by General Shaw Clifton in 2007, will watch the global picture to advise the General on international initiatives that should be launched.

The Army has proved that it can do the impossible: fight successfully on a thousand fronts at the same time. And what it has done in the past it can do in the future. So if the Army remains faithful to William Booth's vision, even a hundred years from now people will still be saying that where there's a need, there is The Salvation Army! Perhaps by then it will not be war on a thousand fronts but on ten thousand!

Ultimately it will depend on each Salvationist personally. Recently in an African village baby twins were thrown through a glass window after their parents had been murdered. 'A poor widow Salvationist happened to be passing by,' we learn. 'She gathered the babies up and, with the help of her corps family, is now raising them. Barely able to feed herself, she is committed to nurturing these two beautiful children for the Lord.'

With that kind of spirit, the continuance of the war on a thousand fronts is assured.

GENERAL JOHN LARSSON (Rtd) was world leader of The Salvation Army from 2002 until 2006. Swedish by nationality, he and his wife Freda served as officers in Britain, South America, New Zealand and Sweden before he became the chief of the staff at International Headquarters. He graduated from London University with a BD degree, and is the author of *Doctrine Without Tears*, *The Man Perfectly Filled with the Spirit*, *Spiritual Breakthrough: How Your Corps Can Grow,* and his autobiography *Saying Yes to Life*. He is a composer of music and, together with General John Gowans, has co-authored 10 full-length musicals.

26

BIBLICAL EQUALITY

MAJOR JOANN SHADE

One approach to an essay on biblical equality is to congratulate ourselves on The Salvation Army's historical commitment to the full involvement of women, while failing to consider Allen Satterlee's observation that, in regard to women, 'it may find itself passed by, viewed as being mired in tradition instead of as a tradition-breaker'[1]. A second tactic is to focus on the Army's 'divided heart' towards its women officers[2], for while rooted in the passion of Catherine Booth for the equality of women, The Salvation Army has wrestled with the role of women in leadership, its varied cultural contexts throughout the world, the challenges of the male/female relationship within its officer marriages, and the wide-ranging ways its own women see themselves in ministry.

Instead, the goal of this short chapter is to raise the questions of where we are and where we're going in the context of an accepted definition of biblical equality, framed by Judges chapters 4 and 5 narrative of Deborah and Barak's leadership. Standing in the first decade of the 21st century, where does the faith and praxis of the Army fit in the discussion of biblical equality in relation to gender? Has there been, as Danielle Strickland suggests, a 'subtle yet increasingly theological and systemic shift' (away from biblical equality)?[3]

Utilising the paradigm developed by Christians for Biblical Equality, the principles of biblical equality are threefold. First, human equality. 'All people are equal before God, and are equal in church, home, and society.'[4]

---

[1] Allen Satterlee, *Turning Points: How the Salvation Army Found a Different Path*, Alexandria, VA: Crest Books, 2004, p10

[2] Carroll Ferguson Hunt, *If Two Shall Agree,* Kansas City, Ms.: Beacon Hill Press, 2001, p150

[3] Danielle Strickland*, The Married Women's Ghetto RANT.* Journal of Aggressive Christianity. Feb/Mar 2006 accessed on 8-25-08 at www.armybarmy.com/pdf/JAC_Issue_041.pdf

[4] Alan G. Padgett, Accessed on 8-25-08 at http://www.cbeinternational.org/new/pdf_files/free_articles/PPWhatIsBiblical.pdf

Galatians 3:28 embodied all people.

The second is equal responsibility. 'Race, gender, and class are not barriers to Christ. Membership, ministry, and mission are open to all in his kingdom, based upon our personal vocation, moral and personal qualifications, and the gifts of the Holy Spirit.'[5] Writing to her fiancé William in 1855, Catherine Booth's words foreshadowed her later determination that men and women should have equal opportunity within the fledgling Army.

> May the Lord, even the just and impartial One, overrule all for the true emancipation of woman from the swaddling bands of prejudice, ignorance and custom which, almost the world over, have so long debased and wronged her... If indeed there is in Christ Jesus 'neither male nor female', but in all touching his Kingdom 'they are one', who shall dare thrust woman out of the church's operations or presume to put any candle which God has lighted under a bushel?[6]

While there is opportunity that comes through the appointment system, there is also a sense of responsibility from the grassroots. It is easy to blame the structure, the administration, or a particular leader for limiting the opportunities for women, in particular, for married women, and at times that blame is justified. Yet there are as many examples of women who are content to fill the second chair role, who don't preach the gospel (except perhaps on Mother's Day), and who are putting their own candle under a bushel.

The third principle outlined by Christians for Biblical Equality is that of mutual submission. 'Christian love is the heart of life in the Spirit. Mutual submission is Christian love in action, treating each person with dignity.'[7] Here is where Salvation Army structure bumps up against the biblical principle. Can 'the commander' truly express and model mutual submission? Can we take a secular, military configuration and live out biblical mutuality, or are the two concepts in conflict with each other?

In Judges chapters 4 and 5, the narrative and song describing the battle

---

[5] ibid

[6] John Waldron, *Women in The Salvation Army,* Toronto, Canada: The Salvation Army 1983, p40

[7] Alan G. Padgett

of Mount Tabor, we do find examples of equality, equal responsibility, and mutuality within a military battle setting, particularly relating to gender. As the Israelites cried to the Lord for help, God brought about their deliverance when they set aside their preconceived gender roles and trusted God for his guidance. As Deborah, Barak and Jael realised, 'On the battlefields, the power of God is not gendered.'[8]

From the beginning of the passage, human equality was modelled by Deborah, as she assumed the prophet's mantle, holding court under the Palm of Deborah, and this equality was accepted by the people of her community. As a married woman, she was leading (judging) Israel, and served her people by resolving their disputes, being a mediator. When the threat of war came, she gave direction to Barak, the military commander, to prepare for battle, and ultimately went with Barak into that confrontation. Deborah moved out of her home and into the greater society, taking her place on the pages of the history of the people of Israel—quite equal with the men of her culture at that time.

In the actions of both Deborah and Barak, we recognise the role of equal responsibility as well. Deborah could have given Barak the orders from the Lord, and then decided to stay under the Palm of Deborah, presumably much safer and more comfortable than the steeps of Mount Tabor. Barak could have summoned up his male machismo and gone on his own, but instead insisted on Deborah's presence (4:8). Together, they led the Israelites into battle.

Regarding mutual submission, both Barak and Deborah submitted to each other's leadership. Deborah went with Barak to Kedesh (4:9), but Barak did the summoning of the other men. Deborah gave the order to go (4:14), and Barak made the advance (4:15). Even the song in Judges 5 that chronicles the events of chapter 4 is one that is sung by both Deborah and Barak.

The week before she died (1890), Catherine Booth called for her husband at 4 a.m. with a solemn message: 'She feared the women of The Salvation Army were not going to rise up to take the place she wished for them.'[9] Carroll Hunt recognises the dilemma:

The Salvation Army legacy as told in literature and history reveals a divided heart when it comes to its women officers, trained and

---

[8] Mitzi Smith, Lecture notes, Ashland Theological Seminary, 8-22-08

[9] Roger Green, *Catherine Booth,* Grand Rapids, MI: Baker Books, 1996, p298

commissioned equally with the men, and at times handed what the Christian world considers 'a man's job' but at other times ordered to stand back and stir the soup, preferably quietly. But the world contains an Army of women warriors called by God to service, and they are not about to disappear by discrimination.[10]

The challenge for today as well as for the future is to reaffirm our missional commitment to biblical equality, and to work towards that ideal in the midst of a fallen yet ever-changing world. To fully embrace our birthright of a theological commitment to the principles of biblical equality takes concerted intention, effort and determination, but as The Salvation Army, sons and daughters of Catherine Booth, we have no alternative but to press on.

This must include:

1. A commitment to teaching, preaching and modelling our biblical and historical imperative of biblical equality.

2. An investment by current Salvation Army leadership in the continued development of its women warriors, and a consideration towards applying the tenets of affirmative action in this area.

3. A movement toward repentance and reconciliation. A well-publicised rally of an American ministry included a powerful display of reconciliation. Prominent pastors stood before representatives of various ethnic groups (Latino, Asian, African-American and Native American), and spoke of the sin of the church against these people throughout recent history, symbolically embracing them in a spirit of reconciliation. One group was missing from their list—women. When one segment of the population is treated differently than the others, there is a need for repentance. When we choose to see each other through proscribed gender roles, we accept the limitations of the curse.

4. An awakening and an arising. In the spirit of mutuality, Deborah, Barak, Catherine and William call for an awakening and an arising among the men and women of The Salvation Army. An awakening among men, to recognise and name the constrictions placed upon their mothers, wives and daughters by years of tradition and prejudice. An awakening among women, to fully accept and live out the call of God on their lives. A rising

---

[10] Carroll Hunt

up of men, to use their power to effect change. A rising up of women, to break free from 'the swaddling bands of prejudice, ignorance and custom'[11], striding up Mount Tabor with Deborah and lifting Jael's tent-peg into the air.

Have we rested too long on the laurels of Catherine and the two Evangelines, amazing and anointed as they were, as proof of our commitment to biblical equality? Are we truly modelling an equality of humanity, equal opportunity and responsibility for men and women, and a mutual submission grounded in love? In the final account, will it be said that on The Salvation Army's battlefield, the power of God was not gendered?

---

[11] John Waldron, p40

MAJOR JOANN SHADE ministers with her husband Larry at the Ashland, Ohio, Ray and Joan Kroc Corps Community Center. She received a BA in sociology, MA in pastoral counselling, and a doctor of ministry degree from a theological seminary in the 'women in prophetic leadership' track. She has served in dual clergy roles in varied appointments of corps and divisional headquarters. She enjoys participating in the creative arts, particularly writing, composing music, poetry and playing the piano. She has written *The Heartwork of Hope: A Directed Journal* and *Seasons: A Woman's Calling to Ministry*, and is a weekly columnist for the local *Times-Gazette*.

27

INNOVATION

COMMISSIONER JOE NOLAND

SOMETHING NEW

Some see things as they were.

Others see things as they are.

A few see things as they will be.

Innovate is defined as introducing, inventing something new or original. Genesis first records the origin, source, creation, or coming into being of something new. 'When God began creating the heavens and the Earth, the Earth was a shapeless, chaotic mass, with the Spirit of God brooding over the dark vapours' (Genesis 1:1–2 TLB). The word *bara* for 'create' means 'give being to something new'.

It has been observed that while we often obsess over history, represented by statistics, such while culturally appropriate can be functionally inappropriate. Creating something new is genesis, which comes before history. *Genesis* is 'finding in the chaos beyond culture antidotes for the stagnation of status quo' (*Orbiting the Giant Hairball*, Gordon MacKenzie).

'YES' TO GENESIS

Status quo is stagnation. In the beginning God was saying 'No!' to status quo ('status no') and 'Yes!' to *Genesis* (creation): sky, land, oceans, plants, sun, moon, fish, wild animals, cattle, reptiles, man, woman. *Genesis* is the spiritual counterpart to innovation (a secularly derived concept). *Genesis* takes the 'No' out of in*no*vation and replaces it with 'Yes'. Allow me to invent a new word here, 'In*yes*vation', which now becomes a modern *Genesis* counterpoint.

Culture is a set of shared attitudes, values, goals, and practices that characterise an institution or organisation. Every new in*yes*vation will ultimately create its own unique culture, appropriate for that particular time, place and setting. As *Genesis* continues to unfold there will be a natural reluctance to embrace and assimilate each new ethos as it emerges, clinging tight to what has now become status qu*no*—'things as they were'. Nostalgia is a powerful emotion, with none of us immune to it. Thus eventually our 'clinging' will be defined by 'an unhealthy refusal to let go of the past', leading to chaos (status quo + innovation = chaos). In other words, 'the enemy is us'.

NOSTALGIA: LONGING

Nostalgia's warm embrace grips me every time I hear this 1969 hit, sung by Mary Hopkins, written by Gene Raskin, putting English lyrics to a Russian song:

> *Those were the days my friend,*
> *We thought they'd never end,*
> *We'd sing and dance forever and a day.*
> *We'd live the life we choose,*
> *We'd fight and never lose,*
> *For we were young and sure to have our way.*

I remember it well, 1969: Beatles, bell-bottom jeans, tie-dye shirts, electric typewriters, pay phones, 35 cent gas, counter-culture, LSD, flower power, free love, Iron Curtain, communism, Vietnam, chemical warfare, race riots, student anti-war movement, Weather Underground, Operation Chaos. Ah yes, 'Those were the days my friend!'

Webster defines chaos as 'a state of utter confusion'. Chaos is the incubator for creativity and innovation. *Genesis* occurs when we say 'No!' to status quo (things as they are) and 'Yes!' to need (things as they will be). Cultures collide. Chaos ensues. Cravings arise.

Genesis is the creative response to our need-based cravings. John Stott said, 'Vision begins with a holy discontent with the way things are.' Allow me to substitute the word 'vision' with the word 'Genesis' in this context.

CULTURE AND CREATION COLLIDE

When Jesus came, culture and creation collided. This was another of those quintessential *Genesis* moments. Jesus invaded 'the chaos beyond culture' with 'antidotes for the stagnation of status quo'. Read the Gospels and you will find that he penetrated the chaos with an exclamatory 'No!' to status qu*no*, and a resounding 'Yes!' to need. You don't have to read far before his clash with the religious culture of the day becomes proactively evident: healing on the Sabbath, touching a leper, speaking to a Samaritan woman, feeding five thousand with minimal resources, uttering a new 'love' commandment (John 13:34)—all need-based. It doesn't get more in*yes*vative than that.

Another of those *Genesis* moments came 1,500 years later when Martin Luther acted on the courage of his convictions, thereby ushering in the Protestant Reformation. 'Here I stand; I can do no other. God help me. Amen!' It takes courage to say, 'No!' and conviction to say 'Yes!' He was later to write, 'Faith is permitting ourselves to be seized by the things we do not see'—or 'see things as they will be'.

GENESIS MOMENTS

The Salvation Army, in its epochal *Genesis* years, dared courageously and with great conviction to sing and dance in the chaos beyond the culture that had spawned its early pioneers (Industrial Revolution). When Catherine said 'Never!' she was saying 'Yes!' to *Genesis* and 'No!' to status qu*no*. This is one of those rare instances where the word, 'No!' is appropriate because, in this case, a 'yes' would be a 'no' to *Genesis*. She was saying 'No!' to culture and 'Yes!' to need.

William Booth said 'No!' to *Volunteer* and 'Yes!' to The *Salvation* Army. This was an in*yes*vative decision, not lacking in courage and conviction— 'seeing things as they will be'.

General Frederick Coutts said during the press conference following his election (1963–69): 'I am going to get with it. Oh my, *YES*. If we want to attract young folk, we have to go where they are, to the coffee bars, to their haunts. I can see us making use of all kinds of music—guitars and banjos, and that sort of thing. If we have to adapt to be understood by the beardies and weirdies, all right, we must. We have to get with it. You dig me?' This was another *Genesis* moment in the life of our movement.

When the training principal said 'Yes!' to a contemporary folk-singing group 'The Salvation Singers' (1964), and to their invasion into the topless nightclubs and hippy haunts of North Beach, San Francisco, this was a

Genesis moment. Subsequently, when a gutsy DC gave me permission to purchase and customise a hearse (1969) for innovative evangelism, this was another of those *Genesis* moments in our movement.

When Eva Burrows initiated the first domestic science teacher training college for African girls, this was an archetypical example of in*yes*vation. Later when, as General, she boldly led The Salvation Army back into Eastern Europe, with work being re-established in the former East Germany, Czechoslovakia, Hungary and Russia itself, this was a spirited, in*yes*vative decision, each a *Genesis* moment in time.

When then Commissioner Paul Rader said 'Yes!', liberating ('to set somebody free from traditional socially imposed constraints') me to expansively plant innovative corps in The Federated States of Micronesia, this was a courageous, in*yes*vative decision opening a series of *Genesis* floodgates.

GENESIS THINKING

The *Genesis* thinker has learned how to separate the 'culturally appropriate' from the 'functionally inappropriate' and say 'No!' to status quo in whatever form it may take: tradition, modernism, oppression, whether it is personally or institutionally driven ('We've never done it this way before'), and say 'Yes!' to conviction, change and emancipation (things as they will be). *Genesis* thinking is exhilaratingly liberating.

Genesis (In*yes*vation) is a future-tense word—'seeing things as they will be' and acting creatively upon that vision—no fear, courage and conviction essential. The best way to teach and empower *Genesis* thinking is to model it. Thus this chapter ends with an appeal for futuristic *Genesis* thinkers and doers. Every ending should always form the *Genesis* for a new beginning, so let this ending begin by restating the opening premise as it is meant to be:

A few see things as they were.

Some see things as they are.

Most see things as they will be.

The genius of The Salvation Army has always been in its *Genesis*—the ability to 'see things as they will be' and then courageously invent, create, in*yes*vate, whatever it takes to reach the supreme goal: 'You are to go into all the world and preach the Good News to everyone, everywhere' (Mark 16:15 TLB). The word, 'No!' cannot be found in this command. Rather it is punctuated with a *Genesis* 'Yes!'—'the creation or coming into being of something'.

'Therefore, if anyone is in Christ, he is a new creation; old things have passed away; behold, all things have become new' (2 Corinthians 5:17 NKJV).

GENESIS IN MOTION

What about the future? The Salvation Army must continually and courageously rev up its efforts to invade 'the chaos beyond culture' with 'antidotes for the stagnation of status quo'—*Genesis* in motion. There are many models to inspire us, General Eva Burrows being one among them. *YES!*

COMMISSIONER JOE NOLAND with his wife served in corps and administrative positions in the USA West, as well as in Australia. He earned his BA and MS degrees, and retired in 2002 as territorial commander for the USA East. Known for innovative and dynamic leadership, he is now engaged in the 'no strings attached' *Genesis* process. His ministry can be summed up in three words: chaos, creativity and controversy—three elements he sees implicit in any successful in*yes*vative endeavour. His mantra reads, 'Creativity is my drug of choice'. He invites you to his website @ www.joenoland.com.

28

GOVERNMENT RELATIONS

MAJOR CAMPBELL ROBERTS

'Government is too big and too important to be left to the politicians.'
—Chester Bowles

The quality of life for every man, woman and child born into the world is impacted by government. Whether it's government springing from the august chambers of the national parliaments of the world or from the informal gathering of local tribal or village elders, government affects people's happiness, freedom, wellbeing and their contribution to their communities and futures.

God is interested in how his human family is governed. There is an obvious and consistent thread woven through the narrative of the Old Testament. God liberating his people from an oppressive Egyptian government, providing the Ten Commandments as a national code of morality, and encouraging his judges to be judicially competent or his kings to be just in the method, conduct and manner of their reign.

In the economy of God the whole of life is important: political, economic and social. Governments and their actions do interest God, for the divine intent is that the universe should be a cosmos not a chaos, with human governance arrangements that bring life, peace, justice and compassion.

The persuasive impact of government on people means that a Christian mission like The Salvation Army must have strategies that allow it to engage and influence government. General William Booth realised engagement with public policy, particularly as it impacted the most vulnerable, was a core business of The Salvation Army. An early example in Booth's ministry of influencing government was the Purity Crusade of 1885. This campaign led to the introduction into the British House of Commons of a massive petition petitioning for the age of consent for women to be raised to 16.

A later example of Booth's engagement with public policy was the 'In Darkest England and the Way Out' scheme. It focused on alleviating poor housing, unemployment and poverty with innovations in areas such as the labour market, emigration, health care and penal reform.

Booth placed such importance on influencing government that he proposed an extensive intelligence department to collect factual information on human and social issues. He realised that government and public policy would only change with evidence-based information from which to root reform.

Booth promoted this 'In Darkest England and the Way Out' scheme in a series of world tours. On each tour he engaged with prime ministers, politicians and other leaders of government. Each subsequent General of The Salvation Army since William Booth has found ways of influencing public policy, usually by direct contact with community and government leaders. Encouragement has also been given to territorial leaders and Salvationists to be similarly involved.

During her time as the international leader General Eva Burrows met with more than 20 heads of state; a wide range of presidents, prime ministers and international leaders, including the President of the United States of America, leaders in Europe, Asia, and heads of African nations.

The present international leader of The Salvation Army, General Shaw Clifton, recently established in New York the international social justice commission to strengthen links with the United Nations and provide resources to international Salvation Army leaders in their connecting with governments on public policy and social justice initiatives.

The biblical antecedent for this engagement by The Salvation Army with governments and political leaders is perhaps best found in the prophetic traditions of the Old Testament. The prophets declare the Word of God in a way specific to the political and governmental context in which they live. Though their contexts are diverse, three consistent themes are common to all the prophets' work: identification, denunciation and annunciation.

IDENTIFICATION

The biblical prophets don't speak from outside of politics or government situation, but as participants in it. They identify themselves, even going into exile with their people, sharing in starvation and deprivation. The prophets experienced the reality of their people's suffering as their own suffering.

At the heart of any gospel proclamation is identification with those who suffer. Gustavo Gutierrez, speaking in a visit to Dunedin, New Zealand in 1986, said, 'How can you say you love the poor if you have no friends who are poor?' For Salvationists, identification means making marginalised people our friends, rather than simply 'doing things' for them.

Being with the poor and the marginalised of the world has been a fundamental prerequisite to Salvationist engagement with governments and public policy. For that task, it is essential to share the life of the poor. Henry Gariepy in his biography on General Eva Burrows records an instant typical of this Salvationist identification with the poor.[1]

> When Burrows made her first visit to Portugal there was a short
> break in the schedule and her hosts offered to take her to see some
> of the historic sights of Lisbon. Burrows responded, 'I am not here
> as a tourist, I am here as a Salvationist. I would like to see the work
> you are doing among the poor and the homeless.'

Gariepy records that the poverty she saw that afternoon affected Burrows and she declared later, 'Not only am I better informed, but I can talk about these programs and help secure needed support.' When Salvationists share with the poor, they can better advocate for them with governments.

DENUNCIATION

The prophets criticised abuses of government and power wherever they occurred. They did so with reckless regard for their own safety. It mattered little to the prophets that they spoke often into impossible situations with nobody listening and nothing changing. Of prime importance was that the Word of God was spoken.

From its earliest days, The Salvation Army has spoken to politicians and governments about social evils that damage and destroy people's lives, denouncing harm caused by poor legislative control on the use of alcohol and gambling, highlighting the destruction caused to people through

---

[1] Henry Gariepy, *General of God's Army*, Victor Books, 1993

prostitution and human trafficking, and pointing to the inadequacy of government policies when they fail to provide the basics of shelter, food and safety.

ANNUNCIATION

Annunciation is made possible by measuring reality against a vision of how things should be. The world is seen not only as it is but also as it might be.

This annunciating voice of the prophets continues to challenge Salvationists today who press politicians and governments to act for those who are vulnerable and without.

Salvationists are painfully aware that the world is fatally fractured. Innocent African women are raped by invading soldiers while Asian and European children go missing and are trafficked. In other societies indigenous cultures wrestle for recognition from their colonisers and the resultant ethnic and sectarian conflicts cause heartache and misery. For many of the world's people, hunger, homelessness and fear rob them of the 'abundant life' Christ offers.

This world needs saving and its politics and government structures need reforming. As a worldwide Christian mission The Salvation Army is called to be a voice for social justice and better government. Finding methods that will effectively engage and influence governments needs the best energy and creative attention that The Salvation Army and its leaders can muster.

Essential to Salvationist methods is credibility. When working in the areas of politics and government, credibility is vital. A Salvation Army with practical experience and well thought through evidenced-based policy solutions will be a welcome voice in government committees, working parties, the news media and other places where the public mind can be influenced.

Salvationist vision for the future needs to be articulated in a way that is meaningful to those engaged in the affairs of government, with words and actions relevant to the everyday affairs of the city or country and strategically targeted to win support for systems of government that reflect God's imperatives of justice and mercy.

Our world is undergoing enormous structural changes, environmentally, economically and politically. Salvationists are called to engage in enhancing the reign of God on Earth by helping governments and leaders reflect the values and ways of the Kingdom of God.

History teaches us that The Salvation Army can influence the world of politics and government. It will need to continue to find innovative ways of interpreting and applying the biblical text to impact how people are governed and how public policy solutions are delivered. General Eva Burrows provides an example of this in her own manner of informed and reflective engagement with politicians and government leaders. She engaged with gentle wisdom, showing immense respect and regard for the people she met with. She spoke the truth without fear or favour and was always clear about who she served. The highest moments of Salvation Army history have been where the Army as an organisation or individual Salvationists have spoken up for the voiceless and vulnerable.

What is important in this generation and at this moment of history is that The Salvation Army is a powerful clarion voice to politicians and governments. If it is, there can be hope that the whole world can be redeemed to be a place of freedom and justice for all the children of God.

MAJOR CAMPBELL ROBERTS of New Zealand is territorial director social policy and parliamentary relations and social programme secretary. He has also served as divisional commander, territorial social service secretary, and is a member of the New Zealand territorial coordination council and the international moral and social council. He is a national media spokesperson on issues of poverty, prison reform, housing, and unemployment, and a member of royal commissions, government task forces and boards, working parties and forums around a range of social issues. A former speaker of New Zealand's House of Representatives said of him, 'Campbell Roberts is the most effective non-party political voice and a leading New Zealand advocate for those on the margins of New Zealand society.' He has co-authored a book on social justice with Captain Danielle Strickland.

29

COMMUNITY DEVELOPMENT

RICARDO WALTERS

Those from among you shall build the old waste places. You shall raise up the foundations of many generations; And you shall be called Repairer of the Breach, The Restorer of Streets to dwell in (Isaiah 58:12 NKJV).

Soap and soup have long been hallmarks of The Salvation Army. One could even be forgiven for assuming they are the very things represented by the iconic 'S' adorning each lapel of every Salvationist uniform. Compassionate social service has certainly characterised the Army in popular opinion—a just-in-time hand-out and hand-up to those who are down on their luck.

But The Salvation Army has long understood that charity and goodwill are simply not enough. Effective warfare by *this* Army requires that conscience and conviction spur us towards social action, where mercy meets the cause of justice in the world. A world where the wealthiest 1% have income equivalent to the poorest 60%; where the combined wealth of only three prominent families equals the annual income of over 600 million people living in the world's poorest countries; where more than one billion people live on less than US$1 a day. A world increasingly crippled by poverty of hand, beaten down and bruised by poverty of spirit.

General Arnold Brown spoke to this global experience: 'The frontline of The Salvation Army must always run through the agony of the world.' How fitting it is then to see that, across the globe, through development projects, The Salvation Army is engaging with issues such as war, human trafficking, child exploitation, healthcare, HIV/AIDS, refugees, environment, water, sanitation, natural disasters to address not only the symptoms but the root drivers of suffering and injustice—poverty, under-developed infrastructure, limited education, unequal power relationships and gender inequity.

In all our collaboration, our best partnerships, our spirit of participation and inclusion, when stripped down is there a peculiar 'Salvationist essence' that can yet be distilled? Certainly we don't have exclusive claim to belief in the right of each person to dignity, not in the secular or the faith arena.

While social action and social justice have characterised our mission from the beginning, in this too we are joined by a host of others working to alleviate poverty, offer access to water and education, to sanitation and housing, to the protection of the most vulnerable. If this is true, what is it about our work in community development that remains distinctive?

Perhaps the distinctive of our practice is best revealed in the light of our theology. That in the midst of brokenness and pain, isolation and abandonment, poverty of hand and spirit; at the desperate edges, the frayed corners, the fragile landscapes of our lives, Jesus himself draws near.[1] Could it be that development is simply the complement to incarnation? People are not alone. They are accompanied in life by the one who is acquainted with grief and sorrow, who himself knows suffering and who comes to comfort and give life that is full, abundant and free. Life is tough; people fall down. But grace makes it possible for them to get back up again, and become so much more than they once were.

The Salvation Army's Wesleyan heritage makes room for this. Prevenient grace—that persuasive and empowering presence of God, gifted to every person from birth to prepare us for new life in him—is the optimism of a loving Father that matches our present-day 'Yes, we can!' Every Salvationist knows this to be true, because this is our story, personal and collective. Had it not been for the Lord by our side—in the good times, and the bad, in the times we reached for him and even during the times we may have turned away—where would we be?

In Naguru, an urban-slum outside of Kampala, we meet Elizabeth. She speaks no English. And perhaps that's a small mercy. Words would be painfully inadequate, language too crude, to convey the depths of grief. But her eyes fill out the nuance to accompany the loosely translated

---

[1] Salvation Army Song Book 'Jesus himself drew near/When alone on the road/ Oppressed by my load/Jesus himself drew near and walked with me.'

conversation. They swim with misty memory, and loss. Already a widow, she has buried every one of her five children—grown adults, their lives tragically cut short in their prime. The agony of longevity, a blessing become a curse: to outlive one's children. But she cannot surrender to grief. There are five grandchildren still in her care. And every day she works at the roadside that winds by the muddy clay wall of their collective home, selling small parcels of fried bananas to earn barely enough to feed them. She bears her suffering with every bit of strength she can muster. There is loss and pain and grief. She treasures her memories in her heart. She will speak of them to all who might listen. When so many around her grow too tired from the weight of mourning to remember what once was—who once was—she is an exception. Memory sustains.

Could it be that 'accompaniment' is a distinct quality that adds dimension to The Salvation Army's work in development? What begins as rapid first-phase relief progresses towards recovery over time, and no-one is left behind. No-one is left alone. Services and commodities without presence are bereft of soul; and after the dust has settled, and many organisations move on, The Salvation Army remains.

Could it be that 'working from strength', not weakness in people—regarding them as lacking or deficient or unable or incapable—is another distinctive? Understanding that God's act of creation bestows each human with the inherent capacity to care, to hope, to relate, to influence, to change? Our most successful work in development has always been when the people themselves are given space to lead. When they are elevated beyond recipients—and we are elevated beyond providers—towards being participants together.

General Eva Burrows displayed keen sensibility around development of the whole person—grounded in mission. Perhaps, most notably, in a time of great reserve and global stigma, in the early days of AIDS, she saw it as a metaphor for the human condition, and mission; endorsing community-driven care and change; grasping the evangelical significance of facilitation, so that care in the home could lead to change in the neigh-bourhood; and astutely seeing networking as opportunity for witness and influence. The Salvation Army in the time of AIDS required extraordinary leadership and vision; General Burrows made it a frontline issue.

Addressing The Empire Club of Canada in Toronto in 1988, General Burrows revealed this intuition for incarnational ministry:

You know, the rough sleepers in London know the Salvation Army officers very well. One of our captains was moving around this night giving soup when he pulled at some cardboard and said 'Tom!' because Tom always slept there under cardboard. 'Tom,' he said, but Tom didn't move. So the captain lifted up the cardboard and Tom was unconscious. Like a good Salvation Army captain, he picked him up and took him to the hospital. Next day, he went back to see him. There, in one of those great big wards like they have in England, he saw Tom as he walked in, and Tom saw him. He said: 'Good morning, Captain. How are you?' The captain said, 'It's not how am I; how are you, Tom?' 'Oh,' he said, 'I'm great, Captain'. He said, 'Gee, thanks for helping me last night. You saved my life. Oh,' he said, 'Captain, I hope you don't mind, but when they brought that form around this morning, I put you down as my next of kin.' I like it. I like it. The Salvation Army wants to be next of kin to the homeless in the world.

We're fighting too in the front line of defeat and desperation with men and women who are intimate with failure and suffering— we're in the business of recycling human beings.

I could keep you here all day telling you about our global mission, the varieties of our service for the disillusioned, the poor, the destitute, the sad, the lonely, the despairing. These are our people and we are fighting to help them.

Finally, I say we are fighting to help people put the spiritual dimension back into life. In this contemporary world of ours, people have magnified the material and denigrated the spiritual so that people are often materially prosperous, but spiritually bankrupt.

The Salvation Army must ever seek to lift development beyond provision, to labour for our work to mean more than commodities and services. Development must be the moral responsibility of those who believe that justification is possible through grace, but must be mirrored by justice; that the glorious hope of reconciliation with God can be mirrored by reconciliation of one man with another; that it can never be enough to redeem the body and lose the soul. Instead, at our best, it is possible to do both. Development that is integral. Integrated. Holistic. A Salvation Army kind of development.

RICARDO WALTERS is a soldier at the Observatory Corps in Cape Town, South Africa. He co-ordinates an all-Africa regional facilitation team under the Africa Department at International Headquarters, offering on-site support to African territories to strengthen their mission responses to HIV/AIDS, and health-related community development. Since 2003, he has applied this experience to work with The Salvation Army and others, beyond Africa, in North America, South America, Europe and the Asia-Pacific region. Ricardo is married to Lisa, and they have a son, Zachary.

30

HOLISTIC MINISTRY

COLONEL HENRY GARIEPY, OF

Jesus Christ calls us to servanthood, to the cross, to participation in what he is doing now in our world. The Salvation Army's theology is a practical theology; it is not solitary but social, not passive but active. It does not segment the spiritual from the social, but integrates the needs of the total person. We acknowledge our pluralistic endowment under God, a synthesis of evangelism and social services, with all that implies. The entry in Dag Hammarskjold's *Markings* is ever timely, 'In our era, the road to holiness necessarily passes through the world of action.'

The word *holistic* comes from the Greek *holos* meaning 'whole'. The word and its meaning have been axiomatic to both our theology and practice. It leads us to focus on the whole person rather than artificially dichotomising him/her into a social and spiritual being. It recognises the interdependence between all facets of the human condition—physical, emotional, intellectual, social, spiritual.

John Wesley, a mentor of William Booth, declared, 'There is no gospel but the social gospel.' Holiness without social concern is as a soul without a body; but social concern without holiness is as a body without a soul. Only when wedded together do we have a healthy, life-giving gospel.

The cross of our Christian faith has two beams: the vertical beam of relationship to God, and the horizontal beam of relationship to others. The two intersect in our Christian faith to provide a holistic ministry, which has ever been a hallmark of The Salvation Army.

Christ does not call us to program, to position, to promotion, or even to production. He calls us to people—in their hurts, crises, deep spiritual needs. The Salvation Army was born a spiritual revolutionary movement, under the dictum of our Founder's motto: 'While women weep...while children go hungry...while men go to prison...while there remains one dark soul without the light of God—I'll fight to the very end!' This is our birthright. These are the fires in which Salvation Army tradition was forged.

In the aftermath of the urban riots of the mid-1960s The Salvation Army launched its Multi-Purpose Center in a riot-scarred ghetto next to the heart of downtown Cleveland. The centre's galaxies of programs and services drew over 10,000 members and more than 1,000 different persons a day coming through its doors.

When Billy Graham came to Cleveland in 1972, he asked to visit the centre. He interacted with the youth and staff in the multiple programs serving the critical needs of that community. Our tour ended in the chapel where I commented, 'Billy, here is the core of this centre where lives have been transformed by the grace of our Lord.'

He observed, 'Henry, this is truly Christianity in action!' I responded, 'Thank you, Billy, for the best definition I have ever heard of The Salvation Army.'

Salvationists have never subscribed to the artificial dichotomy between the sacred and the secular. The time-honored slogan defines its mission as 'Heart to God, hand to man'. Its spiritual and social work are as the two blades of scissors, each essential to provide its cutting edge.

The Salvation Army indeed is Christianity in action, a faith with its sleeves rolled up, out where the air is blowing, the issues are real and people are hurting. It serves as the infantry of the militant Christian church. Though today more sophisticated, its mission remains un-changed—defined by General John Gowans, 'to save souls, to grow saints, and to serve suffering humanity.' We are called to salvation, sanctification and service.

General Arnold Brown threw down the gauntlet, 'The front lines of The Salvation Army run through the agonies of our world.' Where the world is at its worst, there The Salvation Army needs to be at its best.

Today as our multiple ministries encircle the globe in 118 countries, we maintain a vigorous evangelism alongside our practical ministries found at the front lines of human need. General Shaw Clifton reminds us, 'It is part of our DNA to be involved in working for social justice.'

Our human services have expanded exponentially, with response to major tragedies both domestic and international, and with the advent of mega-centres of operation. This poses administrative and financial challenges, but also that of maintaining the primacy of the spiritual, lest we become morphed into a social service agency devoid of our spiritual birthright and mission.

As one of the great leaders in Army history General Eva Burrows transcends her generation. She epitomised Kipling's 'to walk with kings and not to lose the common touch'. She quintessentially modelled the Army's holistic ministry and the hallmarks of an Army, both through the years of her active service, and now in her vocation of 'active retirement'.

As an adjunct faculty now for 13 years at our training college, I am each year encouraged by the next generation of cadets who come in dedication of their entire lives to our holistic ministry. We have moved into a new day of monumental change and challenge. But we have an unchanging, all-powerful Lord who will give us power equal to our tasks.

COLONEL HENRY GARIEPY, USA, is author of 29 books and recipient of the Order of the Founder. Books include devotional, Army history and biography including that of General Eva Burrows, chapters to more than 50 books, numerous articles, series for the Army's international radio program—*Wonderful Words of Life*, *Portraits of Christ* with over 200,000 copies in multiple editions, and he is listed in *Who's Who In US Writers*. Following corps, youth and divisional appointments the Colonel served 15 years as USA national editor-in-chief prior to retirement in 1995. In 1994 he organised the Army's first international literary conference, inaugurated the Crest national book plan, and serves as a Bible teacher. He earned his BA and MS degrees and was honored by his alma mater with its 1994 alumni lifetime leadership award. He is a three-time 26-mile marathon finisher, and with his wife Marjorie takes delight in their family.

31

THE END OF SALVATIONISM

MAJOR STEPHEN COURT

THE END PART 1

THE END OF SALVATIONISM — DESTINY

The title of Roger Kimball's essay in the June/July 2008 issue of *First Things* is 'The End of Art'. 'That is intentionally ambiguous, of course, suggesting that when art has no end, meaning self-transcending purpose, it is the end of art.' (Richard John Neuhaus)

That is to say, if something lacks a self-transcending purpose, that spells its own end. The choice is destiny or demise.

Writing in *Salvationist* in 1879, William Booth summed up our destiny in the following simple but striking way: 'We are a salvation people—this is our specialty—getting saved and keeping saved, and then getting somebody else saved, and then getting saved ourselves more and more until full salvation on earth makes the heaven within.'

FULL SALVATION ON EARTH

This is Salvationism in fullness, leading missionally to Booth's assertion that, 'Salvationism means simply the overcoming and banishing from the Earth of wickedness' (William Booth, *The Officer*, 1893).

The chapters you have read in this volume outline aspects of this greater destiny to win the world for Jesus, to establish full salvation on Earth.

Section 1 of this book emphasises the 'getting saved' and 'getting somebody else saved' components of Booth's explanation of the end of Salvationism. Contributors have tackled this broad issue from a variety of perspectives, each adding a rich understanding of our divine mandate to help win the world for Jesus.

In our early days, the Lord Jesus Christ endorsed this end of

Salvationism. God wrapped a small group of misfits in Holy Spirit conviction, infused them with love, dressed them in prophetic garb, fitted them with a holy disdain for dignified reputation, trained them in the sacrificial Cross-life, deployed them amongst the poor, and transformed peoples of the world.

THE END PART 2

THE END OF SALVATIONISM? — DEMISE

What distracts us from our destiny can spell our demise.

The opposite of 'self-transcendent' in the lead quote above is 'inferior or ordinary'.

There are some dangerous spiritually 'inferior and ordinary' threats to Salvationism. Most appear in insidious fashion to divert us from our commitment to win the world for Jesus. And, yet, if we succumb to their subtleties we could possibly witness the demise of Salvationism. The destiny of Salvationism is:

• not the growth of The Salvation Army (it is much more than that—it is Kingdom expansion to the Revelation 7 depiction of every language, every people, every nation, every tribe);

• nor the protection of our reputation (that may or may *not* be the means— let's concern ourselves with our character and let God take care of our reputation);

• nor the solidification of our finances/properties/investments (it could conceivably mean the liquidation of those properties and investments to pour directly in mission);

• nor the comfort and support of our officers (i.e. limited resource belongs in mission before allowances and benefits; we don't 'coddle the saints' as Commissioner Elijah Cadman preached);

• nor the establishment of our ministerial credentials and place among the churches (though these are potentially useful, we are not here for the group photo);

• nor the clarification of our slot at the top of a bunch of charities (this is not a service club competition);

• nor the imitation of other Christians on trendy theological themes (the goal is not spiritual acceptability within the Body of Christ).

These don't just make a list of potential threats. These are real and active on fronts in different parts of the developed world.

The destiny of Salvationism is not the aggrandisement of The Salvation Army, just as the purpose of General Eva Burrows' international leadership was not the increased fame and favour of General Burrows. We mustn't be trapped in this obvious tactic of the enemy.

What might spell Salvationism's demise, on top of the threats listed in the bullet points above, is the slavish imitation of non-Salvationist theology and philosophy that has seeped into The Salvation Army over past generations. This book, along with a shelf-full of new titles in this latest revival of Salvationist publishing, when embraced, will protect us from potential demise consequential to such enthralment.

Carnality is always a threat. But, praise God, we are part of the holiness movement. We believe that holiness is the solution to every problem. Our embrace of holiness is powerful enough to overcome the potential distraction and demise of Salvationism through friendship with the world, with consumerism, materialism and hedonism.

Hallmarks of The Salvation Army is not merely a celebration of a great Salvationist or a great Salvation Army, it is restatement of who and why and where and how and what we are.

It is a sensitive correction, in cases necessary, of mistaken tactics and strategies.

It is a straightforward clarification of vital truths and effective praxis.

It is a sanctified clarion call forward to the realisation of our destiny— the end of Salvationism—to win the world for Jesus, seeing full salvation on the Earth.

And it will help ensure that none of these potential threats will spell its demise, the end of Salvationism. God help us to stay focused on him and his calling for us.

THE END PART 3

TEAR HELL'S THRONE TO PIECES

The means of realising our destiny—the missional end of Salvationism— is to tear hell's throne to pieces ('We'll tear hell's throne to pieces and win the world for Jesus'—Colonel William Pearson).

Sections 2 and 3 of this book are intended to supply familiarity with the means to our end. They fill in the 'keeping saved' and 'getting saved ourselves more and more until full salvation on earth makes the heaven within' component of General William Booth's definition of Salvationism. Authors for this section help explain how we can most effectively disciple converts toward mission fulfilment and transform our world by full salvation.

Inspired by the visionary example of General Burrows and edified by the excellent teaching of outstanding leaders in the chapters of this volume, how might we most effectively advance toward our destiny, the end of Salvationism? How can we see full salvation 'tear hell's throne to pieces' to 'win the world for Jesus'?

MEANS TO AN END

Let's not compromise on salvation (Mark 1:15,17; repent and believe, follow Jesus). Let's hold to unashamedly Wesleyan holiness (with crisis as a theological necessity). And let's universally embrace covenant, which is potentially transformative (if we do, it will reverse global fragmentation and position ourselves such that God can download his destiny for us).

Let's recognise that 'the fellowship is in the fight'. This is the most robust and intimate kind of fellowship (not to be confused with bland coffee and stale biscuits after the Sunday meeting). Let's guide our war-fighting by the modus operandi, 'capture, train, deploy'. And let's 'love to fight and fight with love'. Why? The love of Jesus in us never fails.

How will we get there, personally? We must be greedy when it comes to the means of grace. Our spiritual rations must be more critical for our health than the food we ingest—we indulge regularly with God through prayer and the Bible. We must engage in discipling—we get trained and we train others to win the world for Jesus. And we throw ourselves into evangelism—this becomes a (super) natural outcome of fruitful discipleship. And all of this happens within the context of compassionate, justice-tinged intentional cultivation of authentic Christian community.

THE END?

These exhortations to warfare in the coming generation provide means to an end—the end of Salvationism. A hallmark is a stamp or mark indicating genuineness, a standard of purity. If these chapters do not closely resemble your experience, then the challenge is obvious. Respond to the challenge spiritually. Allow God to transform you to the point that these hallmarks of Salvationism are also hallmarks of your life and warfare so that you can help fulfil Catherine Booth's foundational prophecy, her imagined destiny for The Salvation Army:

> The decree has gone forth that the kingdoms of this world shall become the kingdoms of our Lord and of his Christ and that he shall reign, whose right it is, from the river to the ends of the Earth. We shall win. It is only a question of time. I believe that this movement shall inaugurate the final conquest of our Lord Jesus Christ.

THE END

MAJOR STEPHEN COURT invests in several initiatives to help win the world for Jesus, including MMCCXX, a plot to see new outposts in 2,000 cities in 200 countries in 20 years; BE A HERO campaign to raise up 10,000 heroes for children-at-risk; armybarmy.com, and Journal of Aggressive Christianity, all while seeking authentic Christian community and trying to incite a Jesus Revolution. He has helped start congregations, corps, outposts, The War College, armybarmy blog, the Booth-Tucker Institute, The War Room and Credo Press. He earned his PhD, has written several books, and since 2007 serves as the training college principal for the Australia Southern Territory. His wife Captain Danielle Strickland and he are raising their boys to be mighty warriors of the Lord Jesus Christ.

SECTION 4

EPILOGUE

32

WITH LOVE, FROM AFRICA

COMMISSIONER HEZEKIEL ANZEZE

I was an officer when General Eva Burrows became the General of The Salvation Army. It was my first experience to see an active lady officer General.

Let me tell you, she became the General of the people. She was my General because she was so close to the people that my heart was touched by her spiritual influence.

Her visits to Kenya helped The Salvation Army in Kenya to be recognised by the government. Her talk to the press was touching and healing to people of Kenya. Our Army was strengthened by her influence during her visits. She was known by the majority of our Salvationists in Kenya.

I remember one time when she was being flown to Kakamega in the western part of Kenya and the pilot lost direction. She saw on the ground people in white uniforms, and she told the pilot that they had arrived and that they should land.

We know her as a courageous leader who was always available for us. Her messages were deep, and delivered in a simple and clear language. The Holy Spirit of God never left her.

It is because of her example that we are now able to appoint women officers in leadership positions.

We still wish her to live longer in order to give blessings to her spiritual grandchildren around the world.

I am happy to be the one from Africa to write our tribute to General Burrows. God bless her.

COMMISSIONER HEZEKIEL ANZEZE is territorial commander of Kenya East Territory, a territory that had grown so large (the Army's largest) that in 2008 it was divided into two territories. His tribute represents the great number of African Salvationists who were impacted for Christ by Eva Burrows' early 17 years of ministry there, as well as by visits and interest shown in later years.

33

FAMOUS LAST WORDS

GENERAL EVA BURROWS (RTD)

(This article was first given as a lecture to cadets in Melbourne as part of a series on 'Famous Last Words', and later incorporated in a book with that title. It seemed appropriate to feature it as the final article in this festschrift on behalf of General Eva Burrows, as a summary statement of her life and faith.)

THE SUPREMACY OF CHRIST

Perhaps I am nearer than I know to saying my last words, famous or not. When I answered a phone call at home not long ago, a rather distinguished voice informed me that he had been assigned by *The Times* of London to write my obituary. To which I indignantly responded, 'But I'm not dead yet.' And he nonchalantly replied, 'Oh, but we have to be ready!'

No doubt he was ready with his obituary. Certainly I can assure you that I am ready—ready for that final home-call from the Lord whenever it does come. I must admit though that I am enjoying Christ's company and being his servant here on Earth so much that I hope *The Times* will need to keep the obituary on file for a long time yet.

Writing your own 'famous last words' is very different and more challenging than writing an obituary. I wondered how I would tackle it, and decided that I might concentrate on the conviction that has developed as I have lived my life under the Lord's influence since I became a soldier of Christ and of The Salvation Army 60 years ago.

My life's conviction, my life theme, has become: in everything, Christ has the supremacy.

That started early in life. I am a daughter of officers; the eighth of nine children. I was born in good Salvation Army style on Sunday morning in the officers' quarters, when my father was leading the knee drill in the hall next door. Always a highly confident child, I innocently thought I was one who was especially loved by Jesus. In my family I was always called Eve, and at Sunday school we used to sing a chorus which I thought was 'I am so glad that Jesus loves me, Jesus loves Eve and me'. Was it an early sign of the pride and self-confidence that was often to trip me up? Certainly I was devastated when, after I had learnt to read, I discovered the words were 'Jesus loves even me'.

Now I know that it *is* a wonder that he loved 'even' me, with all my faults and failings, with all the arrogance and rebellion of my youth, my desire to take my own path of disobedience.

The conviction that my life was no longer centred on my own ego, but on Christ, and on Christ alone, came when as a university student I handed my life over to Jesus. After vowing that I would never go to The Salvation Army, I ended up at a youth councils and finally at the mercy seat. I sought Christ's deep forgiveness, and my spiritual mind-set from that moment was not just to follow Christ, but to identify my whole life's purpose with his—and serve as an officer. And it has been my life's theme ever since.

It was when I was a cadet that I found the Bible verse which expressed my life's motivation in Colossians 1:18 (in those days we used the King James version) 'That in all things, Christ shall have the pre-eminence'.

As I reflect over my life, my appointments and the countries where I have served, I would like to share with you some of the lasting impressions that remain, and they all centre on Christ Jesus.

I was a 23-year-old probationary lieutenant when I went to Africa, an exuberant, enthusiastic missionary teacher. At our mission station, Howard Institute, I was ready to do or die for Jesus, to live incarnationally, to love as he loved, and serve as he served. There I learnt to see Christ through African eyes, and loved him even more.

You can understand why the words of an elderly African Salvationist made a lasting impression on me when he said, 'Captain, if I thought my prayers could be answered, I would pray for you to be black.' I offered those words to the Lord as a gift.

For 17 years Zimbabwe was my home. I never thought I would leave. In reflection I treasure the opportunities that so enriched my life. There I discovered and developed the leadership qualities and gifts which I hadn't known I possessed. I felt so much at home there that when the Army leaders instructed me to leave and take an appointment in London, it was a grief experience. By now I was principal of our girls secondary boarding school. I saw my role as giving African young women the chance to shine in a culture where they were often rated second class, and to find through Christ a life of the best quality.

Everything that happens to us contributes value to life if we know how to use it under the Spirit's guidance. After the simplicity and frugality of life in Africa, it was a struggle for a time to adjust to living in the Western world, but God had lots for me to learn. The lasting impression of my years in leadership at the Army's International College for Officers was the way God opened my eyes to the world-encircling internationalism of the Army. I shared with, listened to and taught officers from every part of the globe. I was at the hub of the Army's world, and at the centre where Army history came alive. No longer was William Booth just a figure of history, but very real. I absorbed something of his spirit and passion for souls, his care for the disadvantaged, and for the extension of our movement to every corner of the globe. Among my last words, there will still be, 'Christ for the World: the World for Christ'.

No matter how much of life's experience and wisdom you may have gained, you can still get surprises. Big surprises! After thinking that my future as an officer would be in the educational field, and rather looking forward to that, there came a bolt from the blue. At least a bolt from the General, who appointed me in charge of the women's social services of Great Britain. What is the Lord up to here? I wondered. I was pretty soon to find out that Christ's bias for the poor went far beyond the disadvantaged and needy of Africa, to the last, the least and the lost of the marginalised in the crowded cities of Britain. It was an illumination: his deep love for the poor, the abandoned and the unloved permeated my soul with a passion that has never left me, and will colour my life on Earth till I die.

As I look back, my next move was also unexpected, an appointment to Sri Lanka for my first territorial command. What lasting impressions were made by my years there where I was faced with leading our Army in an Eastern culture? I discovered a new dimension to life, serving where there were strongly entrenched non-Christian faiths. Learning to respect the sincere believers of the Buddhist, Hindu and Islamic religions was bringing me to a new awareness of the uniqueness of Jesus Christ. Imagine my surprise when, invited to present a Christian 'thought for the day' on the English radio in Colombo, I discovered there was a 'thought for the day' by each of the four religions. Fortunately I was able to listen to the four broadcasts for a few weeks before it was my turn. As I listened it seemed to me that there was little difference between them, for mostly they were a series of admonitions on how to live a good, religiously moral life in order to please God.

Reflecting on this challenge to my participation, I realised in a new and meaningful way that what Christianity had to offer was not an introduction to a set of ethical rules but an introduction to Jesus Christ himself, the living Christ. He is not dead like the Buddha or Mohammed, and he does not merely show us the way; he *is* the way. Yes, I had known that as a theological truth, but now like an incandescent light it came to my soul with new realism and power. That is what I must proclaim. From that time on I have said that I do not preach Christianity, but I preach Christ—our glorious Saviour and Lord. That I will do till I die.

Not long after that experience in Colombo, I was having lunch in the home of a wealthy Indian, and was impressed by a magnificent painting on the wall with the portraits of Moses, Buddha, Jesus and Mohammed. In answer to my questions about its origin, he said he had paid for it to be painted because, though he was not a follower of any religion, he admired all four. They were the founders of the great faiths of the world, and he saw them as of equal value to mankind. I concurred with his first point but then, with courtesy, told him why I could not agree with his second point, explaining that Jesus Christ, unlike the others, rose from the dead and lives to walk with us along our journey of life. This confirmation of my 'thought for the day' experience was another reminder that the resurrection of our Lord is not just an important theological tenet, but the key to our faith. The crucifixion and the resurrection are essential aspects of the one mighty redeeming act of Christ whose saving grace triumphed when he rose from the dead. My 'famous last words' might even be, 'He lives. My Redeemer lives.'

Among the lasting impressions of my life at this time was my first attendance at a high council to elect the next General at Sunbury Court.

I was the newest territorial commander there, rather over-awed by the many, high-powered Army notables present. My feeling was that it would be best for me to listen and learn and say nothing, sitting as I was at the end of the line of seniority. At the close of the first session I was staggered to be called up by the president of the council, who said he wished to appoint me the chaplain of the high council. I had the temerity to say, 'But Commissioner, do you know I am the youngest and least experienced leader here?' His gracious reply was, 'My dear Colonel, spiritual authority does not depend on age or experience.' It was a lesson that I took seriously to heart, and put into practice.

After gaining practice as a territorial commander in Sri Lanka, the General appointed me to command The Salvation Army in Scotland. My lasting impression there was the first serious illness of my life. I suppose when we are always healthy, we never think we will ever be unwell. So when I suffered a heart attack, it was a great shock. News flashed to international headquarters, and even around the world, that this promising woman leader had passed away. But God had other plans. When I woke up in a hospital bed after emerging from sedation, there was a black nurse sitting by my bed, and I thought I was in Africa. When the nurse turned out to be one of my former students at Usher Institute who was studying coronary nursing care in Glasgow, I knew that the Lord was graciously looking after me. So after a time of recuperation, I was back on duty, and enjoying my service among the ardent and enthusiastic Salvationists of Scotland.

The next stage of my life was a return home to Australia. After 31 years of officership in many parts of the world, this was my first appointment here. The Lord calmed my fears, and I was amazed at how quickly that inner adjustment mechanism got into action. I felt at home right away. I'll never forget how pleased I was when, after giving a talk at the meeting on Christmas Day at the old Gill Memorial hostel for homeless men, one of them said to me as I shook his hand, 'You talk real ocker, you know.'

But then haven't we found that we can feel 'at home' anywhere and everywhere when the Lord is with us?

Pretty soon I got to know the Army in Australia, being able to call soldiers and officers by name. That's when I got the reputation for having a good memory for names. It wasn't really a memory for names, but a memory for people. In my life Jesus comes first and people come next.

What I wanted most of all was to lead the territory after the style of Jesus Christ. Was that too simple an ambition in a modern, sophisticated Western territory? My introduction of church growth programs was not to use some popular technique to grow The Salvation Army, but as a way to introduce Aussies, often cynical about Christianity and the Church, to Jesus Christ himself. My passion to give unemployed young people a chance to learn job skills and find hope for the future led to Employment 2000. My ardent speech at the taxation summit in Canberra was to highlight our motivation and Christ's mission through this movement. But my lasting impressions of those years are the miracles that Christ brought into the lives of people by his Spirit, and how he leads us forward to accomplish his will and grow his Army through its diverse ministries.

In 1986, at my third high council attendance, my election as General changed the whole course of my final years of active officer service. A lasting impression of those years is the constant sense of privilege I felt at being granted this role as Christ's servant. You'd never take the job on unless you believed God had placed you there, and you can only do it in his strength. For me those seven years encompassed the challenge of returning to the lands formerly dominated by the communist, atheistic philosophy where The Salvation Army had been banned for so many decades. It led to the restructuring of the administration of the Army in the United Kingdom and globally. It allowed me opportunity to develop the training in leadership of officers from the areas or Asia and Africa who would soon take positions of responsibility in a wider, multicultural leadership of The Salvation Army.

My brief included travelling to all corners of the world to visit, to preach, teach and inspire our people. It was with quiet delight that I heard an African Salvationist say in his words of thanks for my visit, 'General, you are our global parent.' The congregation gave him a wild round of applause. Yes, I thought, our Army is one Army, one great family crossing all national and cultural boundaries. One in Christ. On the screen of my mind flashed the sight of a mercy seat, in the shape of a massive cross, in the arena of the Royal Albert Hall in London at the international congress meeting a short time before. At that cross were kneeling 'a great multitude of every nation, and tribe, and language', hundreds of Salvationists in every style and colour of uniform, kneeling by the cross of our Saviour and Lord. Christ has the supremacy in The Salvation Army.

To recount the lasting impressions of those years would take a book in itself. But most impressive of all were not meetings with kings, queens or presidents, but the beautiful, unforgettable Salvation soldiers of the cross whom it will always be a joy to reflect on until I greet them again in glory. Salvationists like CSM Thankimah in East India, who began life selling watches on the streets of Aizawl. Now, prospered by the Lord, and owning a magnificent business, he spends his wealth paying the salaries of couples to evangelise in unreached areas of his country. Or YPSM Clara Page, an exuberant African-American of South Carolina, whose organisation of a Sunday school of over a thousand, young and old, was magnificent. She told me how she passionately longed for all to come to know her Saviour. Or Major Yin Hung Shun, who led our Army in China after the forced expulsion of our missionaries. His endurance under the cruel conditions of a communist labour camp during the cultural revolution made him into a hero of the faith and an inspiration to me and the whole Army world.

But life doesn't end at retirement from active officer service; lasting impressions continue to mount up; open doors of service for Christ continue to open. I am now an active soldier of Melbourne Temple 614 Corps, where we are concerned for the lost, the last and the least in this inner urban area. I see as many miracles on Bourke Street Melbourne as I saw in the villages of Africa, or the hostels of London, or the streets of Colombo. I have had the exciting task of preparing young men and women to take their place in the ranks of the Army as soldiers, ready to make the values of the kingdom of Christ and not the values of the world the standard for their life, to fight passionately against social injustice, and to seek to win the world for Jesus.

No wonder I hope *The Times* of London does not need to publish my obituary just yet. But whenever that day does come, my last words will be that Jesus Christ has ever been the supreme and passionate love of my life. I have earnestly endeavoured to centre my teaching, and preaching, and serving on him, though it has been so imperfectly. Now I await with patience the golden dawning, when I shall behold him face to face.

THE PEOPLE'S GENERAL

GENERAL EVA BURROWS (RTD)

Eva Burrows was born in Australia, the daughter of Salvation Army officer parents. She committed her life to God for service as a Salvation Army officer while studying at the University of Queensland in Australia and, having gained a bachelor of arts degree, entered the William Booth Memorial Training College in London. Commissioned a Salvation Army officer in 1951, she took a course at London University to obtain the postgraduate certificate in education.

Having sensed a compelling call to serve in Africa, she was appointed as an officer teacher to the Howard Institute, a large mission station in Rhodesia (now Zimbabwe), which hosted schools, a teachers' college, a hospital and a training college for Salvation Army officers. She developed a curriculum for training of native teachers in the network of Salvation Army schools throughout Zimbabwe. During her first homeland leave she undertook study at Sydney University for the degree of master of education, and presented her thesis on the training of African teachers in Zimbabwe. She subsequently became a consultant to the national educational department on the development of school curricula. She was appointed head of the teachers' college and then vice-principal of the Howard Institute before being appointed principal of the Usher Institute, an educational establishment for girls. Under her innovative leadership, the institute became well known in Zimbabwe as an outstanding girls' educational centre.

After 17 years in Africa, in 1970 Eva Burrows was appointed to London where she spent five years at the International College for Officers, first as vice-principal and then principal. In 1975, she became leader of the women's social services in Great Britain and Ireland.

In January 1977 there began a period of 10 years of territorial command. First was Sri Lanka where she immersed herself in the life and needs of the Asian people, introducing new schemes and programs. At her departure, an editorial in *The Ceylon Observer* commented, 'We say without fear of contradiction, that people like Eva Burrows grace any country they serve in.'

Her next command was in Scotland for a further three years of inspirational leadership prior to taking command in 1982 of the Australia Southern Territory. There, innovative initiatives characterised her leadership over the next four years, including an imaginative program for unemployed youth, and the introduction of church growth principles and concepts.

On May 2 1986 the high council elected Eva Burrows as General and world leader of The Salvation Army, taking office on July 9. As General, she gave spiritual and administrative oversight and direction to the worldwide movement. Her five-year period in office should have ended in July 1991. However, by overwhelming vote of senior international leadership, she was extended to serve an additional two years, retiring in July 1993.

During her first five years as General, Eva Burrows visited 62 countries, and was translated into 41 languages. These overseas campaigns were not only a source of inspiration to Salvationists throughout the world but enabled the General to make contact with people at all levels of society, from hostel residents to heads of state and government.

In 1990, as General she convened and presided over an international congress that brought to London Salvationists from every continent for 10 inspiring days of celebration and discussion. She also initiated and sanctioned a far-reaching reorganisation of the administration of the movement, both internationally and in the United Kingdom. Perhaps most significantly of all, she led The Salvation Army back into Eastern Europe, with work being re-established in the former East Germany, Czechoslovakia, Hungary and Russia.

General Burrows has been honoured with a number of honorary degrees, including an honorary doctor of philosophy from her alma mater, The University of Queensland. However, such has been her willingness to spend time with individuals whatever their status that she became known as 'the people's General'.

She retired as the world leader of The Salvation Army in July 1993 to live in Melbourne, Australia. In the Australia Day honours list in 1994, she was appointed a Companion of the Order of Australia. She has many invitations to speak throughout Australia and around the world, but one of her priorities is her faithful service in the local corps, including its mission to homeless youth.

Her home territory, Australia Southern, and the worldwide Army join in November 2009 in thanksgiving, prayer and celebration of 'what God hath wrought' in and through her life and mission these 80 years.

Notes